What people are saying about *The Pretend Christian: Traveling Beyond Denomination to the True Jesus* by Deirdre Reilly

"Doing a show about Christ, I've been introduced to every denomination out there, and I've been thrilled to see people unite when discussing the stories of Christ, and dismayed to see them divide when insisting on their denominations. This is a great book at the perfect time, and more than that, it's IMPORTANT."
Dallas Jenkins, Creator, "The Chosen" streaming television series

"*The Pretend Christian* introduces the reader to the reality of relationship over religion. A 'now generation' message of great value; a pearl of great price."
Alveda King
Evangelist, director of Civilrightsfortheunborn.org

"Deirdre Reilly really hits the heartbeat of the Christian journey with her new book, *The Pretend Christian*. This is a must-read for having a real walk with the Lord. I love Deirdre's point of view, and her seriousness in declaring that if we as Christians say 'I'll pray for you...' we need to mean it. Your faith will be increased after reading *The Pretend Christian*."

Pastor Mark Burns
Named by TIME Magazine as "Trump's Top Pastor"
Named "One of the 16 People to Have Shaped the 2016 Presidential Election" by Yahoo News

"The reader is immediately taken with author Deirdre Reilly as she describes her compelling faith journey. This book is refreshing, honest, forthright, and engrossing."

Kathleen Kennedy Townsend
Former lieutenant governor of Maryland and author of "Failing America's Faithful: How Today's Churches Are Mixing God with Politics and Losing Their Way"

"I loved reading *The Pretend Christian* by Deirdre Reilly. She writes authentically about the ups and downs of her spiritual journey that reflected much of my own experience. This is a book worth reading by anyone who is not sure about their faith, or for anyone who has questions and doubts, but still wants to know and experience Jesus."

Skip Vaccarello
General partner with 1Flourish Capital, author of "Finding God in Silicon Valley", chairman of Connect Silicon Valley

"In *The Pretend Christian*, Ms. Reilly convicts Christians to critically examine their behaviors to see whether they are drawing others to Christ or pushing them away. More importantly, she challenges non-believers to look past those behaviors and through to the overwhelming love in the heart of God Himself."
Meg Meeker, MD
Best-selling author of "Strong Fathers, Strong Daughters"

"In *The Pretend Christian*, Deirdre Reilly has given us all a great gift. Through a captivating narrative, she describes her own search to understand faith and the twists and turns of life. In reading the work, I found myself laughing, getting choked up, nodding my head in approval, pausing to reflect, and just feeling good about a real and honest account of the struggles and joys of life and faith. If you're looking for candor and a sincere heart, this book has both! I strongly recommend it!"
Fr. Jeffrey F. Kirby, STD
Pastor and author of "Thy Kingdom Come: Living the Lord's Prayer in Everyday Life"

"Deirdre Reilly shows the beautiful, but at times challenging, reality of what it means to be a 'real' Christian with a real faith in Jesus Christ. Her stories allow us to peek into her sensitive heart as she discovers Christ as a compassionate and loving friend who wants to share everything with us...Reilly invites all of us to put on our spiritual sunglasses and keep our eyes open to see God's loving activity in us and around us. Wherever you are in your journey, this wonderful book will inspire you to want to know and love Jesus more, and to trust in his tremendous and very personal love for you."
Fr. Michael Sliney, LC
Chaplain, Washington DC at the Lumen Institute

"*The Pretend Christian* is both down-to-earth and profoundly wise. Deirdre Reilly leads us through her own very real and human journey while teaching lasting lessons about faith and Christianity. She is a joyous companion along this path!"
Maureen Mackey
Writer, editor and web content strategist; former editor-in-chief of LifeZette

"Deirdre Reilly has found the secret to an abundant life, and she shares her story in *The Pretend Christian*. It's a story of grace and victory that so many of us need. In a world that often leaves us feeling isolated and cynical, the truth Reilly shares provides a window to where hope may be found."
Seth Barnes
Executive director, Adventures in Missions

"Deirdre Reilly's writing voice is that of a dear and trusted friend. *The Pretend Christian* is her love letter to God and to the Anam Cara, or 'soul friend' that dwells in the heart of every seeker and believer. This little book is a bracing, candid, but also deeply humorous work of pastoral theology and spiritual direction, written in the tradition of Merton, Nouwen and Dorothy Day. Reilly shows us that the voice of God can be heard as a roar or as a whisper, in a messy kitchen while surrounded by dirty diapers or while standing face to face with God at the top of Mount Carmel. All we need to do is listen. *The Pretend Christian* is a book worth reading."
Gerard O'Sullivan, Ph.D., CEO of Corvus Education, LLC and visiting professor of higher education at Wilmington University

"In a world that is desperate for change, this wonderful book, *The Pretend Christian*, shows the reader that we are all walking the same path and struggling along the way. It is a wonderful reminder that we are not alone, we can be great, and it is okay to believe. The net result is a better world for all."
Toni Brinker
Founder and CEO, One Community USA

"My friend Deirdre Reilly's wonderful book is mainly for two kinds of people: Those who know Jesus Christ as their savior and those who don't but who need Him. Deirdre has been in both places, on the hard days and the not-so-hard days, and her genuine faith, understanding and caring shines through on every page."
Mark Tapscott
Editor, HillFaith blog

The Pretend Christian

TRAVELING BEYOND DENOMINATION
TO THE TRUE JESUS

Deirdre Reilly

CrossLink Publishing
RAPID CITY, SD

Reilly/CrossLink Publishing
1601 Mt. Rushmore Rd., Ste 3288
Rapid City, SD 57701
www.CrossLinkPublishing.com

Ordering Information:
Quantity sales. Special discounts are available on quantity purchases by corporations, associations, and others. For details, contact the "Special Sales Department" at the address above.

The Pretend Christian / Deirdre Reilly. —1st ed.
ISBN 978-1-63357-312-3
Library of Congress Control Number: 2020934404

First edition: 10 9 8 7 6 5 4 3 2 1

For my sons, Fred, Matt, and James, and for Matt's new wife, Alexa—my irreplaceable, irrepressible purveyors of wisdom, agents of change, and messengers of joy

Don't judge a man by where he is, because you don't know how far he has come.

—C. S. LEWIS

Contents

Preface

The final push to see this book through to completion came to me one hot summer night as my husband, Fred, and I were sitting on our screened porch. "I'm not fit to write this type of book," I said to Fred, sighing. I had just finished the first draft, and a heavy fog of doubt was settling on my tired mind. "I'm not good enough."

I was despairing. I hadn't attended church in weeks, Fred and I had had a rare, prolonged quarrel that day, and I felt that in one way or another—even if just small, easily forgotten ways—I was letting people down, people I loved and cared about and were responsible to. Why should anyone listen to *me* about faith? My husband's answer was thoughtful and clear. "This is exactly why you need to write this book," he said. "You are good enough, even when you're not."

He was silent a moment, gathering his thoughts. "There are people out there who feel the same way you do every day of their life. They will investigate or deepen their faith as soon as they get their lives together, or when their schedule opens up, or when they are a better person."

My husband was right. In a very informal survey of a handful of friends and family, I had recently asked for a one-word response to two words: *Christ* and *religion*. The answers were very revealing. When it came to Christ, the words offered back were *grace, Savior, Messiah.*

Interestingly, the one-word response I got again and again to the word *religion*? *Guilt.* One friend said, "I curse, I can carry a grudge, and I could be a whole lot better at taking care of myself. Religion reminds me of all the ways I don't measure up." Another said, "I don't know my way around a Bible; I can't even find the separate books of the Bible. I have what you might call a questionable past; I know God would disapprove. That's what the word religion reminds me of."

Imagine a close friend saying to you, "As soon as you get your act together, call me. As soon as you can come over at least one hour a week, call me. Then we can really get this friendship going!" Well, that's no friend at all.

Whether it is scriptural misunderstandings or our own history with religion that's led us here, many of us haven't felt good enough for a true, deep, intellectual, emotional, and spiritual friendship with God or his Son. Or, we haven't ever known how to begin a search for the true Christ. Or, we honestly think it's just a lot of hooey.

Guess what? You are good enough, and so am I. No matter what state we are in. Right now—right this minute.

When I was little I often pretended to be a cowgirl, riding an imaginary horse for hours in our backyard. To me, I *was* riding a horse. Of course, when I grew a little older and rode a real horse—felt the strong animal's movement, heard the drumbeat of his hooves, felt the wind on my face—I could see how far from reality my pretend riding had been. Although my pretend riding served an important purpose, it wasn't even close to the real thing.

To find out how I went from an intellectual understanding of Christ—a pretend sort of faith—to an intimate, ongoing friendship, an eternal relationship that continues even when I don't measure up, read on. I'll give you a hint: it wasn't in a particular church worshipping in a particular way that brought me home; it was beyond human dogma and included several Christian denominations. My journey was, and is, both unbelievably freeing and profoundly humbling. It has given me a way to live an amazing, meaningful life; one far happier than I could have ever imagined.

I have included "takeaways" at the end of each short chapter for both the person open to searching for Christ and for the believer who seeks to deepen their personal relationship with him.

Let's get going!

CHAPTER 1

Can Religion Cause Rashes?

Wherever you are right now in regard to faith, I've been there myself. At different times in my life I've had no faith, very little faith, or confusion and insecurity about certain aspects of any faith I did feel. Most of us have been taught that faith is important. But when the rubber meets the road in our lives and we need to reach into a reservoir of belief, whatever faith we have often doesn't sustain us, improve our situation, or save us.

Why not? Maybe because we are looking at everything the wrong way. Perspective is very important in the area of belief, as is the baggage of personal negative experience and the very human tendency to doubt, to demand proof. Throw in the misinterpretation of scriptural teachings and the disappointment in public and private figures who say they are Christian but act in ways that prove otherwise, and it's no wonder we often feel, in the final analysis, that we are alone.

But we are not alone. There are reasons we feel the way we do; however, they don't diminish or prove false the reality of God or of Christ. If we spend some time unpacking why we can't seem to establish a direct line to God, maybe we will find a life-saving, life-changing surprise along the way.

A very dear friend recently visited my home for the weekend, and she enjoyed some reading in our guest room Saturday morning while I snoozed away in my bedroom down the hall. Later, over a leisurely coffee in the kitchen, I looked with interest at what she was reading, some sort of philosophy book. I asked my friend about it, and she told me that the book discusses belief systems that use trite phrases to convey their most powerful messages and tackles the question of how authentic these religions can, in fact, really be. A lovely, kind, intelligent, and well-educated person, she was careful with her words, not wishing to offend me (she knows I'm a Christian), and I listened with great interest—and deep understanding.

How well I remembered the way my skin would crawl, back in the old days, when I would hear what I considered sanctimonious and insincere Christian turns of phrase, often delivered as throwaway lines—as if the person wasn't really even thinking about what they were saying. "We'll be praying for you!" one person would say to another in the church vestibule, hurriedly putting on their coat while reaching for their smartphone, never even making eye contact. Hearing the phrases "blood of the Lamb," "born again," "have a blessed day," or, "we fellowshipped together" made me feel the same way—itchy. What did any of this really *mean*? It seemed more exclusionary than welcoming, a language only these "churchy" people knew.

It seemed, to use another cliché, a bit "holier than thou."

When someone says, "We'll be praying for you," what they're communicating is, "I will appeal directly to the Creator of the universe, the maker of heaven and earth, on your behalf." That is serious business and a serious promise. How, then, is this phrase tossed off multiple times a day by so-called believers? These religious phrases, as well as others, would literally make me squirm and itch, as if I had a rash. And they shut down any interest or inquiry on my part, because I wasn't privy to this "secret language." Contradictory messages abounded within Christianity, in my experience. God is all about love, we are told, but only if you act a certain way, talk a certain way, believe a certain way. There was absolutely no chance I was going to feel God's love for me when the need for a secret language, among other things, automatically shut me out.

Other examples of "exclusionary" behavior that turned me off for several years to further inquiry into Christianity readily come to mind whenever I ponder this topic; perhaps you have experienced something similar.

First, however, a side note: I have come to understand that many times believers don't realize that they are being exclusionary. They have perhaps gotten used to hanging out with each other too much, comfortable in the company of those who believe and express that belief exactly as they do. While this close relationship is extremely comfortable, spending prayerful time together and enjoying the kinship and even approval of one another, it isn't all we are called to do. Being able to worship with others who believe as we do is a blessing of true faith. It is not, however, the sole purpose of faith. The purpose of worship is to spend time with God. In the worst cases, a "Christian" really does feel they are somehow morally superior to others. Now, that's a whole other ball of wax!

Consider another example of this exclusionary behavior, one that really left its mark on me. When I was about nineteen, my parents were attending several different Protestant churches, and were on fire with their faith. (My folks had each been raised Southern Baptist but had fallen away from any form of church worship as my sister and I grew up and returned to active worship only in my later teen years.) One particular church felt like home to them, and they eagerly participated in their services and programs and longed for my sister and me to do the same. We, however, felt very differently; we hadn't been raised going to any church (except for attendance with each set of grandparents during childhood), and we were almost adults, intent on mak-

ing up our own minds about important things. (We did sometimes agree to go along with our parents to services, though. I remember jerking awake during Sunday services after nodding off,
having sometimes had a late night out partying with friends the
night before. My sister would laugh silently at me as I struggled
to remain conscious during worship.)

One evening during a college break in my sophomore year,
my mother struck up a family conversation at dinner; she wanted my sister and me to attend a teen meeting in another church
member's home. A kindly, older couple who always greeted my
sister and me in a friendly way when we did attend church was
hosting the get-together, so I grudgingly said I would attend.

My sister had a work commitment (lucky for her, I thought),
so she couldn't go along. I was on my own. *Great.* A dentist ap-
pointment for multiple root canals sounded more appealing than
this teen get-together.

One week later, as I walked into the hosts' modest house a
few blocks from the church, I was struck by how peaceful the
home felt; comfortable older furniture graced rooms dotted with
oil paintings, wooden crosses, and other Christian imagery, as
well as framed family photographs. From the kitchen came the
smell of coffee and cookies, and I saw a group of teens—the
same group I often saw hanging out together in church—sitting
in a circle on an oriental rug, laughing and kidding around with
one another. Our host introduced me to the group, and I looked
around uncertainly. What in the world would I have in common
with these kids?

Several smiled openly, inviting me to grab a seat in the rocking
chair at the edge of the rug, while others looked at me through
questioning eyes, as if I were an interloper who threatened their
small, comfortable group.

Unfortunately for me, the first thing on the agenda was a game
called "Bible Trivia." We were to separate ourselves into two
teams and answer different questions about the Bible. "Okay,"

I thought to myself happily, "my team can kind of carry me on this; I will sit back and watch, and have a few of these delicious cookies."

But just then, one of the older teens (I was the oldest of the group, I surmised) said, "Why doesn't each team member answer a question, and then it's back to the other team for a turn, and so on."

I groaned inwardly. *Come on, team, you're supposed to carry me!* I knew a little about Noah's Ark—there were two of each type of animal on it, right? And Moses—he seemed like a good guy; he brought the rules for life carved on tablets down from the mountain, didn't he? I quickly scanned my memory banks—was he in the first part of the Bible, or the second part, where Jesus was the main character? That old itchy feeling began as I sipped my coffee, but the teens around me looked thrilled. They just couldn't wait to get going! Several grinned weakly at me, as if they didn't expect too much.

They were right. As each teen rattled off the correct answer to their question, high-fiving and cheering as they went, I realized these kids had spent a lot of time in church and with their Bibles.

It was finally my turn to answer a question for my team: "What does the first part of the well-known Bible quote John 3:16 say?"

You might well have asked me for the chemical composition of the moon's surface. I realized that it was idiotic for me to be there and pointless for me to be playing this game. I had zero knowledge of the Bible, except to know that you could usually find one in a hotel room dresser drawer.

The group of kids all stared at me expectantly. I shrugged defensively and laughed. "I literally have no idea," I said. "That's all I've got!"

Several of the teens shot knowing glances to one another, a few rolled their eyes, and our kind hosts rushed in to distract me from the kids' rudeness and my own ignorance. I could feel the judgment and derision from the teens around me, and my face grew hot with indignation. *Who did these kids think they were, to judge me?*

This is the type of behavior that brands Christians as acting morally superior to others, even though they are called to be humble and even meek. Now imagine I weren't a teen playing a simple game, but someone in real physical, emotional, or spiritual trouble. Suppose I walked into a church, disheveled and late for the service, desperate for answers or some small measure of God's love. Probably, impatient glares or curious stares from those in the pews, if I did not know the prayers or hymns but instead sat numbly, would not only chase me right back out through the church doors, but would make church—and God—the last place I would ever again go for help, repentance, and love.

My parents and the hosting couple were very disappointed in the teen group, and I never returned to their meetings. They had made me feel stupid, foolish, and "lesser," and I sure wasn't about to go back for more. The experience did, however, cause me to look up the first part of John 3:16, my failed question. "For God so loved the world that he gave his one and only Son, that whoever believes in him shall not perish but have eternal life." Sure, it was beautiful and even poetic—but what the heck did it mean?

I would like to add that those teens turned out to be loving and committed spouses, parents, and community members, and grew out of their "biblically superior" attitudes once they left the cocoon of teen worship groups and entered the real world. I ended up being married in their church, and several of the church members came to my bridal shower and gave me thoughtful gifts for my new home. The "Bible Trivia" experience did, however, destroy any interest I might have had in looking into faith. This brings up the special duty and obligation people of faith have to consider what it may be like to question, and to doubt, and to treat others in that space with respect.

The famous Indian activist Gandhi was reportedly interested in Christianity at one time, but was turned away and called an ugly racial slur when he tried to worship. This caused him to utter the famous quotation: "I like your Christ. I do not like your Christians. Your Christians are so unlike your Christ."

Takeaway for the Searcher

Humans are fallible and sometimes fall very short of modeling the true Christ. That's okay; we are all human. Keep going and keep questioning—you have every right to be in the place you're in when it comes to spirituality. God will meet you there.

Takeaway for the Christian

It is important to remember that you never know who might need your best example of Christ's love and acceptance. The person in front of you could be only a few steps away from making a life-changing decision about faith, and humility will be more helpful than your being overly confident in what is best for them.

CHAPTER 2

What Keeps Us Away

I think that as we begin to consider Christianity, it's helpful to take a look at the things that chase us away from an exploration of the faith—those things that put a bad taste in our mouth or turn us off completely. I have experienced most of these at one time or another, so it's an area I'm familiar with!

I mentioned the holier-than-thou attitudes of some believers as a negative, along with the secret language they sometimes use to communicate. It can sound like spiritual Morse code. *Beep-beep-beep,* they seem to say, *isn't it just awesome?! We understand what life is really about. It's a shame they don't believe!*

Another thing that drives people away from the faith is powerful public figures who claim Christianity only to fall very short when it comes to even basic morality. When I was growing up, it was televangelists Jim and Tammy Faye Bakker, who made millions off of their followers while living in absurd luxury. Jim Bakker even ended up doing some jail time for accounting fraud and also paid hush money to cover up an alleged rape. Other bad examples include far-right "Christian" sects like Westboro Baptist Church, who misquote the Bible to advance their extreme bigotry and hatred against almost everybody, including war veterans, or Catholic Cardinal Bernard Law, who failed to remove and report sexually abusive priests and allegedly covered up their illegal, heinous actions for years. All faiths have issues with human frailty, sin, and leadership failures. Is it any wonder that someone who hasn't been exposed to Jesus Christ's message says "forget it" after seeing how rotten faith leaders can act?

Another claim against Christianity is that it is "simplistic," almost akin to a fairy tale. I believe that is because Christianity has been around so long that people tend to boil it down too far: essentially, *God loved the world even though he caused a flood that killed everyone, then he made rainbows a symbol, sent some rules, and then his Son came down to save us.* Now who could take that seriously? But ask the average person without a scriptural background to describe Christianity, and you will probably hear something similar. In reality, though, Christianity is anything but simplistic. Many martyrs have given up their lives for the faith. It is the world's largest religion and over 2000 years old. If you are dismissing the possibility of God and believing instead only in the power of humanity, consider what many of those humans around the world believe.

An additional argument against Christianity is very popular today: the charge that Christianity is intolerant. In society currently there is a focus on LGBTQ rights, a lifestyle the Bible does not sanction. (For the record, neither do any of the other large world faiths.) I am not a Bible scholar and can only share my experience and my life in regard to this issue. While I used to have strong opinions on this matter, I feel that today God has asked me not to focus my work and my life on this area, but instead to focus on his love and grace for *all* people. That is what I believe he offers, regardless of your race, color, socioeconomic status, or sexual orientation. I have gay friends whom I treasure who respect my faith, and I am comfortable with my stance on this issue.

Another charge against faith is that the Bible treats women as second-class citizens—which is factually untrue. Women are main players in the story of the Bible and deeply important in the story of Christ. Mary, Jesus's mom, is venerated by Catholics and loved by every denomination of the Christian faith. She endured more than any mother should but stayed true to God and to the message of her son's life. Women have been faith leaders, teachers, missionaries, pastors, and lay counselors, and their importance to the faith community cannot be overstated.

Another argument against Christianity that more science-minded people grab onto is the lack of evidence. *Where's the proof?* doubters ask. I like the phrase "absence of evidence is not evidence of absence" when it comes to the "lack of proof" argument, and there is more on this topic a little later in the book. Suffice it to say for now that evidence of God is all around us, but are we looking for it with the right eyes, in the right way? Are we defining *miracle* correctly?

Yet an additional argument against the Christian faith is spread through a willing obtuseness about Christ. "Christian theology is incoherent to the point of absurdity," writes one author on the Atheist Alliance International website. "God killing his son so he can forgive our future sin is like me breaking my son's legs so I can forgive my neighbor in case she ever parks her car on my drive. It is quite ridiculous."[1] But this argument and others like it is silly, because it does not treat Christianity with the respect it deserves. Even nonbelievers can frame Christ's sacrifice correctly; God loved the world and his creations (us) so much that he sent his own Son down to try and teach us about love. Jesus was killed for it, after taking on all of humanity's sin and acting as a living sacrifice. Far from silly, that is a profound and complex idea that even Bible scholars never tire of pondering. The atheist author's snide equivalency is both wrong on its face and intolerant of those who hold the meaning of Christ's crucifixion dear.

Another reason that people turn away from the idea of God is because they have been personally hurt or disappointed by a church or its leader, or their prayers have gone unanswered. These are difficult situations, and totally understandable. I can relate to being disappointed by a church. I was baptized Catholic, and I live in Boston. Here, an evil scandal regarding abuse perpetrated on innocent children by priests was uncovered in 2002, revealing lives shattered and trust betrayed. Catholics worldwide have endured scandals, and we now know that many young people have been sexually abused by priests. This idea—and its cover-up by the hierarchy—is so abhorrent that parishioners have felt personally hurt by it. I myself, as a mother of three boys, was hurt, disgusted, and deeply disappointed. I have to remind myself that my faith is in Jesus, not in humans. Church is a place to worship, not the focus of worship.

And what do you do if you have prayed and prayed for recovery from an illness or addiction in either yourself or a loved one and have received for your troubles nothing more than "radio silence" in return? What if you prayed for a loved one's health and they died a painful, prolonged death anyway? What if you have prayed for your life to truly begin, and for doors of opportunity to swing open, only to have them slam shut in your face again and again? First, I acknowledge and respect your pain, if this is you. How hard it is to live in a spiritual echo chamber, feeling that your earnest pleas to God have not been heard! I have been there, and I understand it. I will say that God *has* heard your prayers and is *right now* acting on them. A little further along in this book you will read about a friend of mine whose faith actually grew through a sudden and shocking tragedy that should have derailed her. So to you I simply say, *hold on*. Breakthrough is coming.

Takeaway for the Searcher
Acknowledging the arguments against Christianity is no threat to confident Christians, so if you need to, explore these doubts with them through discussion. But keep an open mind and ask God to lead your efforts at clarity.

Takeaway for the Christian

The faith is increasingly under attack from intellectualism and our cynical age. If you know someone investigating the faith and feel led to pray for them, stop everything and do it. We need to stand up for what we believe while listening carefully to those who have been wounded by religion.

CHAPTER 3

A Pastor Calls Out His Flock

Now for a positive story about believers! On the flip side of my "Bible Trivia" disaster, I had a unique experience years later that more than countered it, illustrating the humility and self-awareness that really accountable believers can possess. It also opened my eyes to the amazing gift a spiritually aware pastor, priest, or minister can bestow on their church community when it comes to exclusionary behavior: deliver a resounding wake-up call about "churchy" exclusivity.

One Sunday morning years ago, I decided to attend the local Baptist church in our town. My husband and my two oldest boys were sleeping in, so I took my youngest son, then two years old, along with me. I knew that this particular church had a nursery, and I could participate in the service without worrying that he would cry, spit up, or create "interesting" sounds and smells during the service.

I walked into the church to see groups of people standing and chatting with one another here and there around the room. A greeter told me where the nursery was, and I soon had my little one deposited in the bright, book-filled, kid-friendly space with the assurance he would be well cared for.

I came back to the main part of the church and slid into a nearby pew without recognizing any of the faces around me. I looked at the bulletin and visitor card tucked into the back of the pew in front of me—did I want to fill out the card, or remain incognito? I slid the blank little index card back in the pew, putting on my spiritual "dark sunglasses" and remaining unknown to those around me.

The pastor came out, some hymns were sung, an opening prayer was said, and the worshippers settled back, ready to receive the pastor's message. What came next was mind-blowing.

"As many of you know," he began, "I took a trip to the California coast last week for a conference." He shook his head slowly and reflectively, gathering his thoughts. "And I am sad to say that during my flight, through both deep thought and prayer, I realized that this congregation is just not measuring up to even the most basic of Christian ideals. And I, for one, am deeply disappointed—in my own leadership and in you."

You could have heard a pin drop. My mind perked right up. This wasn't a sermon you heard often—this pastor was calling out his flock! I listened with interest, in the unique position of having no emotional ties to the people in this church. Also, I didn't go to this church, so he wasn't talking about me! I could sit back and wait for what happened next with complete impunity.

The troubled pastor continued, "During my flight, I came to the harsh realization that we socialize only with each other. We have turned into a club whose membership is closed. We visit each other when we're sick, or depressed, or need a helping hand, but to others who worship differently than we do, we turn a blind eye. Why? Because we don't even know them."

He made further revealing observations. "Why, I have friends at the Universalist Unitarian Church, as well as friends who don't even believe in God, who are sitting at strangers' bedsides, or bringing meals to neighbors when they're sick, or mowing lawns, or raising money for good causes, and most of all, fellowshipping with anyone, regardless of their church or faith," he continued. "Can we honestly say the same about ourselves?"

This was *really* getting interesting! These folks were getting reprimanded! I stole glances at the people seated around me. Some squirmed uncomfortably, some stared straight ahead, stone-faced, and some nodded their heads in agreement. He was getting through to many of these folks while some, it was clear, were resisting. "We must change," he said, staring out over those seated before him, his expression serious, his tone somber. "We are not doing God's work by staying insular and, I dare say, even 'clannish.' We are with one another only; we don't even bother to reach out anymore. We need to leave the comfortable, safe walls of our church and reach out to others, care for all the needy in our community regardless of what church they attend, and welcome the stranger in our midst into our church and into our lives. If we are to do God's work, we must model his Son's life, as best we can. Many times our job is, as the old newspapermen used to say, 'to comfort the afflicted and afflict the comfortable.'"

What happened next was equal parts humorous and touching. Here, I was a visitor and therefore a stranger to these churchgoers on this particular Sunday, a day when their pastor had given them a good dressing-down about their own exclusivity. So, who was the natural object of their immediate and overwhelming desire to reach out to others? Me! So before I knew it, I had a line of about fifteen people waiting to introduce themselves to me, ask me about myself, and invite me to coffee hour. After about ten minutes, my hand aching from being gripped enthusiastically by others, I excused myself to go collect my toddler.

I smiled as I walked down the hallway to the nursery; this flock's reaction had been swift and decisive. They were ready to change. . . Was I?

As I drove home through my leafy neighborhood, I thought about my own actions when it came to reaching out to others beyond my social circle. I had often told my husband that I longed to donate more money to charitable causes when we had more expendable income. But God doesn't ask you to wait until your bank account is stable; he asks you to do what you can now, to-day. And I hadn't gone to the most recent middle school PTA event when parents of students who were bussed in from Boston were to be introduced and welcomed. I could have, but I had decided to watch a reality TV show instead. Where was my heart for the stranger then?

One of the most important things we can do is to socialize with and love people who worship differently from us, or who have no faith at all. We are all God's children whether we recognize it or not; let's behave that way.

Another thing to remember: it can feel completely over-whelming to believe that you and you alone are responsible for your own destiny and happiness. This is how nonbelievers often feel. It is so important to model God's love for humanity by being open to others who don't share your faith. True evangelizing means, sometimes, not pounding someone over the head with God's message, but instead offering to listen, to empathize, to love. Jesus himself spoke in relatable parables, instead of blasting people with a cold scroll of rules and regulations. Let God come *through* you; others of all faiths—or no faith at all—will notice. The longing may already be there, and your job is not to get in its way. Your job is to help turn longing into action and hopefully action into belief. You won't change the nonbeliever; God will. You may just be one small part of their journey.

When I ponder believers' attitudes toward others, I often think of choirs. Have you ever noticed that all types of top musical acts (pop, jazz, country, rock, and even rap) will occasionally add a choir to a performance? Why is this? Because there is something about a choir—God's music—that touches hearts the way nothing else can. A choir's authenticity calls to us as humans; we are reaching for glory together when choirs sing. We are in the realm of emotion, not intellectualism, and not rules. If followers of the faith are also authentic, they will touch hearts and minds. The longing to reach for something far greater than ourselves has been woven into our human nature by God. In a way, genuine Christians offer "previews" of the type of acceptance and love Christ readily offers; we should try to act as kind and joyful examples of his true nature.

Takeaway for the Searcher

A true believer can be one of the most honest people you will meet, one who is interested in self-improvement and deeply concerned about the welfare of others. Don't let those who profess the faith but act in ways contrary to it, no matter how well-known they may be, hinder your journey.

Takeaway for the Christian

A critical self-examination is an important part of the experience of true faith. Don't rest on your laurels. Keep improving, growing, and putting yourself last when it counts. You never know who is watching, but you can bet God is.

CHAPTER 4

Trapping God in Church

As I mentioned earlier, I spent time with believers growing up, even though during my childhood my parents took a break from formal religion to re-evaluate their beliefs. This foundation, laid when I was a small child, bore fruit much later on. I do remember, particularly in my teens, being comforted by my extended family's somewhat mysterious faith. "They know who they are," I would think and wish for that same type of peace and certainty for myself. I began noticing in my late teens that their faith allowed them true freedom; they weren't using up their precious years on earth wondering obsessively about the point of their lives, which gave them the personal bandwidth to serve others in ways both large and small.

My relatives on both sides of my family tree are solid, active, personable Southern Baptists. My paternal grandfather, James Purcell, was a pastor and missionary in Florida who worked with the very poor and once shared a revival tent with Billy Graham. On my mother's side, my uncle Gerald Primm was a noted pastor in Greensboro, North Carolina. Most members of my extended family have been true believers for as long as I've known them, pursuing lives full of purpose. They're also some of the funniest, most down-to-earth people I've ever known; the dinner table was often crammed with family members wiping away tears from their eyes after a funny story or joke was told.

None of my grandparents was ever wealthy or even well off; they never owned their own homes. But the homes they did live in were always tidy and welcoming to friend and stranger alike. Beloved in their communities, they were well-known and often sought out for their advice on all sorts of matters. My mother's mother, Treva Primm, was a particularly gentle, loving person. She also was an advocate for all races, colors, and creeds—anyone was welcome at her table. Why? Because that's how Christ was. She didn't spend time talking about true hospitality; she lived it.

I remember so clearly being a small child and following her one day into her downstairs bathroom to give it a brisk cleaning. As hot water swirled around the old tub, mixing with powdery Ajax cleaner, she perched on its edge, looking at me with her sparkling, dark brown eyes, a question forming on her lips.

"Do you know that you have a best friend that you can't see?" she asked me, smiling softly, framing her thoughts for a child's mind. "His name is Jesus, and you can talk to him any time you like, tell him anything that is on your mind—things you are happy about, or sad about, just like you would to your mom or your best friend you can see. He wants to know it all."

Later, she showed me a picture of this mysterious Jesus. He was surrounded by children of all colors who smiled up at him trustingly, lounging in his lap or perched at his feet, and he looked like there was nowhere else he would rather be. This was the kind of adult I could get behind! Because my grandmother, someone whom I loved, admired, and trusted, introduced me to Jesus, my first exposure to him was a warm one.

My grandparents never pushed, never demanded, never goaded us into belief in God. Although they saw us only a few weeks a year, they carefully and gently laid a foundation, delivered with love and modeled by action, day in and day out. They brought us to their church, proudly introduced us to their friends, and created opportunities to meet other children raised in faithful households. My grandparents never coerced or chastised my parents either, that I knew of, even during the years my parents fell away from God. My grandparents instead remained confident in God's plan for us and knew they didn't have to do all the work themselves. They could rest easy, trusting that God would do the heavy lifting.

Can you imagine being confident enough in God's power to let go of the reins a little in your own life? *If only,* you might now be thinking—the attempt to control every aspect of our lives is at first tempting, then exhausting, and ultimately impossible. Can you imagine having a positive, hopeful, trusting attitude about faith? Maybe not. I don't think we have even begun to realize how our cynical age affects us. While we are praying or worshiping in church, we feel confident and we believe. Our God is an all-powerful, loving God who works everything together for our good, we affirm aloud. God never ceases watching over us and even knows the number of hairs on our head. Then, perhaps we go out to breakfast. Through a quick check of our social media feeds or through the conversation at the table, we learn of a murder, a terror attack, or more political strife. We all shake our heads and agree, *this world is a dangerous place, man. Better watch your back. . . Poof!* God has somehow left the equation. We left him back in church or our bedrooms, trapped behind our physical walls and our human susceptibility to darkness.

I noticed that my grandparents found happiness in the smallest things because *they focused* on those smallest things—little flowers blooming in the cracks of the sidewalk, a good, ripe tomato, the breeze from a fan gently blowing, and little cards and letters from me and my sister, scrawled painstakingly in an effort to send our love across the miles. My grandparents used not just their faith and their intellect but their *will* to stay focused on God. And God, in turn, perpetually strengthened their will. In our modern age, in which the internet, social media, and TV constantly claw at our minds and our time, can we say the same about our focus?

I thank God for the humble, funny, "faith-on-fire" people I come from on both sides of the family—people who took any opportunity they were given to share their faith and their belief in God's extraordinary mercy and love. Anyone was welcome at their door, and their sterling characters and untold kindnesses lived on after they were gone.

It's funny—as a teenager I remember thinking, "Each of my grandparents talks so knowledgeably about books, the arts, politics, their community, and the world at large. How is it that these intelligent people believe in a God they can't see?" I felt at the time that it was perhaps the only part of their lives where they had been misled; they had "drunk the Kool-Aid" of a too-simplistic faith passed down through the generations, just like so many others.

Then during my later teens I began to notice something, although at the time I didn't give it a whole lot of thought: The natural world had an artistry, a pattern—or more correctly, a seemingly infinite number of patterns—that exuded creativity, a *loving* creativity. A cat's perfectly symmetrical stripes look carefully designed, for example. A bird's wings efficiently allows it to soar, dip, and land with grace, as if created by a thoughtful, exacting engineer. The moon hangs elegantly in the sky, and the beauty of a field of sunflowers has inspired artists for centuries as they try to catch the sheer magnificence of the natural sight. Further investigation reveals even more wonders: A fox uses the earth's magnetic field for direction, even the smallest insects have camouflage to strategically protect them, dolphins have their own sophisticated language, and a sea otter's nose and ear flaps close when it swims underwater, allowing the animal to transition there seamlessly. What caused these intelligent, gorgeous, efficient designs?

Or *who?*

At the same time, I was also aware of this life's great tragedies. Why did natural disasters happen? Why were there wars that killed good people? Why did babies die, and why were children molested and murdered? Surely a God that created such awe-inspiring natural beauty and showed such love for the natural world would never allow humans—whom he claimed to love so much—to suffer like this. The idea was unacceptable.

Additionally, there were religions to explore that offered fewer complications and seemingly more gratification. For example, one friend I knew was deeply interested in Buddhism, based on moral precepts only. Another friend was Jewish, and her spiritual routines and beliefs, rooted in just the Old Testament, were both comforting and appealing. There was always atheism, too, in which life could be lived without responsibility to any certain deity, spiritual code of conduct, or set of rules. Christianity offered too many complex, competing arguments, one being a seeming inconsistency that God so loved us that he gave his Son's life for us, but then nevertheless left us to face life's brutal slings and arrows alone. It made no sense and closed the door to further inquiry throughout my college years.

There was one time, however, during my college years that I desperately reached out to this God I didn't know. I was in school in New Mexico and had gone through an unexpected and difficult romantic breakup as well as tremendous stress surrounding my academic major. I felt like I was on a very small boat adrift on a great sea, experiencing what I now believe was classic depression. I was unable to gather the will or interest to attend many of my classes, socialize with my friends, or even answer the phone. I really just wanted to sleep.

One day I dragged myself out of bed, threw on a sweatshirt and jeans, and began walking towards campus. I had no books and no destination. I could feel tears brimming, and my chest ached with suppressed emotion. Other students walked by purposefully, books under their arms, clothes washed and hair shampooed. What in the world was wrong with me? Why couldn't I handle my own life?

I kept walking and suddenly remembered that there was a Catholic church nearby. I would go in and sit, and maybe God, if he was up there, would notice me and give me a sign, or show up as a ghost or spirit—or however it was that he revealed himself to us mere mortals trapped down here.

I entered the church and sat in a pew in the dark in the back, staring at the giant wooden cross hanging above the altar. Who was this mysterious Jesus, really? How could he possibly help me when I couldn't seem to want to help myself? If anyone was going to love me, wouldn't it be me?

I thumbed through a hymnal, my heart pounding, and suddenly a priest came out of a door to the right of the altar and noticed me. He began walking towards me, stopping to bow slowly and reverently in front of the altar. "Can I help you?" he asked as he walked towards me, squinting in the dim light of the church.

"I...I don't know why I'm here," I said, fumbling over my words. "I'm...lost, I guess you would say, and I'm just so tired. I really think I might need some help." Tears rolled down my cheeks, and my hands clenched the pew in front of me until my fingers were white. I wanted to throw up.

"Have you been to Health Services for the exhaustion?" the priest said gruffly, frowning at me. He sat down next to me on the pew, sighing. "You're not pregnant, are you, young lady? Too many students are engaging in careless sexual activity these days." He peered at me intently, his face drooping into a disapproving scowl.

I swallowed hard, shook my head, and, mumbling apologies, stood up and took off. So much for God, I thought, and how much he cared about his children down here in the messy soup of real life.

Takeaway for the Searcher

Need a place to begin your journey? Think about your favorite things in nature, and then really examine them; get as close as you possibly can. Is that wondrous beauty and exquisite functionality really just an accident—or did a loving God create it, in part for your enjoyment?

Takeaway for the Christian

Remember that people are more important than symbols. Like the priest who bowed at the altar but was dismissive of a student in need, that person in front of you *contains Christ within them;* treat them that way.

CHAPTER 5

Can You Trust Emotion?

Every person who has ever investigated Christianity soon understands one thing: in the end, you must believe by faith. Wow, that's a tough one! Faith is a supernatural experience; it can't be proved, in the sense that many would desire. For those who insist on tangible proof, this often stops any further investigation. Many are distrustful of the invisible, mystical nature of faith and the Trinity of God, Jesus, and the Holy Spirit. If asked, however, many people would probably readily say they believe they have a soul and a conscience—but you can't see or prove the existence of those, either. The only "proof" available is an encounter with a person whose love *from* God and *for* God shines brightly and undeniably through their very being, and through all that they are able to change or accomplish in their lives.

We often have complex, multi-layered, vividly realistic dreams when we sleep, and technically those aren't real—we weren't *really* standing in the swimming pool talking to a circus clown, or sliding down a bannister made of Jello, or being chased by a dragon through an elementary school cafeteria. But we all accept as fact that although they are mysterious, dreams are a real phenomenon, based on our own experience and our shared human experience of them. They *do* happen. So is a real, *supernatural* experience with God that unreasonable?

Human beings are complex; we want documentable proof of the important things in life, but also long for mystical experiences. Once we do get that mystical experience, however, doubt often takes over, and we begin explaining it away. The Holy Spirit is a conduit for experiencing the mysterious, mystical part of God. The Holy Spirit, together with God and his Son, Jesus, allows human beings to experience for themselves the reality of God and the reality of Jesus as his Son. The Holy Spirit can be confusing to understand and very hard to explain. Even longtime believers can be stumped when asked to explain it.

Here is a simple explanation that will perhaps be of use as you ponder the reality of a Holy Trinity, one of the foundations of the faith. The Holy Spirit clarifies, illuminates, and personalizes God and Jesus. The Holy Spirit also empowers us. If you've ever been struck by a Bible passage and feel it has unique resonance in your life, whether you're a believer or not, that is the Holy Spirit, personalizing that message just for you. In the Bible, when Jesus was being baptized in the Jordan River by his cousin, John, God's spirit came to Jesus as a dove, empowering him to begin his mission on behalf of humanity. This was the Holy Spirit, God's spirit. Jesus then immersed himself in humanity and all its cares, even while being part of the Trinity. It is a mystical, supernatural thing, and sometimes hard even for religious scholars to wrap their minds around.

Scholars aren't the only ones. I am reminded of a little boy who would exclaim the incredible nature of the Holy Spirit while I'd be driving my car. As a toddler behind me in his car seat, my third son, James, would often put his tiny, chubby hands to his forehead and say, "I will be with God forever and ever in heaven—I just can't *think* of it!" (Back then, adorably, he pronounced *think* as *frink*.) My own soul would swell as the child I so loved felt God's boundless love. The joy in his soul was palpable, and

I can still see his baby teeth and his happy grin as he expressed this "Holy Spirit" joy.

Sometimes, God delivers the truth of his existence like a laser beam. Many who have had a near-death experience, or NDE, for example, see a glimpse of heaven and are instantly changed into people of deep faith. Others, on the other hand, slowly investigate on their own, begin to pray, and at a certain point believe that everything they've learned is, in fact, true. What a moment that is! As the old hymn "Amazing Grace" says, "*How precious did that grace appear, the hour I first believed.*"

It is not enough to *intellectually* understand God and Jesus. You must *believe* and take that much-discussed leap of faith with your whole being. Not just with your intellect, or your willpower, or your heart—all the facets of the one and only unique *you* must be in balance and engaged in the spiritual relationship. Like other human relationships you have, that's what makes it real—when *all* the parts of you are engaged, and you have employed trust. You will then be truly connected to God, and his love and intimacy will be astounding. (Like any relationship, it isn't always easy, though, and you will struggle sometimes.)

Someday, you may ask yourself how God can possibly deal with you while he deals with billions of other people. You will learn that God cares about your little prayer of frustration when you're late for work and can't find your car keys at the same time he can hear an entire nation mourn after a natural or man-made tragedy. He can in fact listen to and act on the weighty prayers for the sick and dying from all over the globe, from every pocket of humanity, simultaneously. He is not constrained by space, distance, or time. Amazing! That's all well and good, I used to think, but he still isn't provable; I'll never really know until I die if it's all true. Have you ever felt the same way?

I have in the past been a bit wary of the emotion that comes with certain expressions of faith. I am one who likes solid, empirical proof. Take, for example, televangelists, weeping and perspiring and swaying on stage, apparently in a Holy Spirit fever, while asking for your money. Or even my own stirring from somewhere deep within when Christmas music like Handel's *Messiah*, "Silent Night," or "The Little Drummer Boy" is playing. Sure, I would think, I feel something, but that is exactly what that music itself is skillfully crafted to do, make me feel something. I would wonder, is that "something" a divine tap on the shoulder from God, or just music's normal eliciting of emotion? (You can see that I often over-thought things; a friend once told me I would pull a beautiful flower up out of the ground to examine its roots.)

One summer when I was very young, about seven years old, I was seated in my grandfather's small, humble church in the tiny town of Bell, Florida, ready for his Sunday evening service. My grandmother sat next to me, cooling herself with a paper fan printed with Bible verses, and my little sister, Carole, then about five, sat on her other side. Women in hats and gloves and men in suits filtered in, smiling at my grandmother as they settled in their pews. I was proud of my grandparents—my grandmother was loved and respected, and my grandfather was a trusted spiritual leader.

My grandfather had a guest pastor this one particular summer evening. Dressed in a white suit, pale blue shirt, and white tie, this guest pastor was dashing and charismatic, and from the moment he began speaking, my child's mind was unusually alert.

Back then, a lot of what came from a Southern Baptist's pulpit was fire and brimstone warnings of hell. My grandfather's face would often turn purplish-red as he exhorted the faithful to be ever-watchful against the snares of sin, and this guest pastor was no different, to begin with. But then, like my grandfather often did, the guest pastor began to talk of a loving God, a God who wanted to know and love *me*, individually. According to this stranger, God was literally waiting for me (I pictured him drumming his fingers on the arm of his golden throne) to let him know, by walking down to the altar, that I was ready to repent of my sins, submit to his loving will, and experience his grace.

My soul swelled, and I felt pulled by some sort of force to the altar. My whole being wanted to run full speed down the long, carpeted aisle, straight into God's loving arms. I wanted to lie down in front of the pastor and my grandfather, who was seated in a chair behind him, and just cry, because I felt so full of possibility, longing, and urgency.

The feeling was overwhelming. But I couldn't run down that aisle. Instead, I stayed glued to my pew, fighting this incredible, supernatural pull. It would be disloyal to my grandfather, whom I loved so very much, to have a visitor be the one to save my soul. "I'm sorry, God," I prayed. "I can't run down there to you, because it needs to be my grandfather's words that pull me to you, and not this stranger's." My heart was engaged, but my mind was resisting. Later, during my searching years, I thought, "I'm so glad I didn't run up there, swayed by that pastor's persuasive and emotional delivery, and hurt my grandfather by sidestepping him while accepting Jesus and God."

Further along on my journey, my thought was, "How thrilled my grandfather would have been to see his grandchild run up the aisle to accept Christ, the Christ he loved so much, right there in his church!" Later in my life—35 years later, to be exact—God fulfilled my wistfulness around that long-ago event through my third son. My parents were leading a small group within the church they were attending and asked if anyone wanted to come up to the front of the worship space where they were standing and pray with them, releasing the cares of their hearts either aloud or silently, my parents standing by for support. After their invitation to join them in prayer, I was amazed to see my own little boy, James, just five years old, wriggle out of his seat and run up the aisle to them, asking if he could pray with them. I can still see his little blue jeans and orange T-shirt as he ran, arms outstretched towards the grandparents he loved. It remains one of my parents' dearest memories, and one of mine, too. God fulfilled my old longing through my precious little boy, and, I felt, honored my loyalty to a beloved grandfather.

For a short time, I attended a multi-denominational church in Maryland whenever I was home visiting my family. The church was very heavy on "produced" segments during services —funny skits, professional altar lighting, original music—even the preaching was theatrically presented, with soft lighting pooling around the pastor as he spoke and mood music quietly playing from somewhere offstage. The whole package was a sight and sound to behold and urged an emotional response from those in attendance. I always felt a bit uneasy about the level of production involved, even as my imagination and emotion were drawn in by the displays on stage. My grandmother, the former pastor's wife who was at that point in her eighties, completely blind and living with my parents, commented only, "They are a young church." My concern was that the theatrics of the service were touching hearts and minds, but not God's word. Church often seemed less a time to worship the Creator and more a time to immerse in "lights, camera, action." Indeed, the services were so carefully and professionally orchestrated that most attendees would often have tears rolling down their cheeks, hands held high in affirmation. But was that emotion elicited by God or rather this Broadway-type production?

Later, that same church endured a painful scandal, and many left, shocked and betrayed. All the fancy lighting and clever skits in the world couldn't replace humble leadership and a focus on straight-up worshipping God. Today, I believe that God can use anything we experience, good and bad, to draw us to him. I recognize spiritual music as a very effective tool God uses to reach us, and I consider the performing artists and the creators of this music—as well as books, plays, and paintings that speak to the spirit—to have been inspired by God himself. As long as God and Jesus are center stage, you can't go wrong. I guess you could say

I've just learned to relax about it all, stop analyzing everything so much, and appreciate things for what they are. No more pulling up flowers to examine their roots!

Takeaway for the Searcher

God can bring the deepest wishes of your soul full-circle, fulfilling your longings years after you first have them. Also, overthinking can kill experience; in our increasingly cynical world sometimes you may want to just relax and roll with it!

Takeaway for the Christian

If you are lucky enough to be an influencer in someone else's pilgrimage, don't "overproduce" your offerings. If Christ guides your efforts, whether you are in a cathedral or in a wooden hut, he will shine through you.

CHAPTER 6

A Spiritual Dangle

After I left college, I met my husband, Fred. It happened on Saint Patrick's Day in a pub called Lucky Ned's (I now call it Lucky *Fred's!*), and before we knew it, we were in love and getting married. We were also expecting our first child, and although the pregnancy was unexpected, we were out of our minds with excitement to become parents.

I would drive to and from my job at an insurance agency in my little white Volkswagen Beetle during that pregnancy, my heart bursting with love for the child I was carrying, my mind full of plans for our little family's future. The theme from the old *Peanuts* cartoon, a lively piano piece, played often on the radio around that time, and tears of happiness would often spring to my eyes as I anticipated meeting my baby.

Around this time, I became firmly entrenched in "the middle place" of faith—interested to know more about God but besieged by doubt, left in a spiritual dangle. Children often bring about a search for spiritual truth; the serious responsibility of bringing up a kind, moral person can hit a new parent like a ton of bricks, and it sure did for Fred and me. So, one day very soon after our first baby was born, my new husband announced, "We need to start going to Mass for the baby."

What the heck did he say? Prior to having a baby, we had never discussed going to church, although we both came from families that did and affirmed to each other that we believed in the *concept* of God. Now Fred was saying that he wanted to start going to a Catholic Mass? I had never even been baptized! I had gone along to Mass when we had visited his family, and considered it sort of an aerobic workout, with all the kneeling, standing, and sitting. And their prayers were long and odd, to me.

"Hold on a minute, mister," I said. "This is a decision we make together. I don't know if I want our kids to be Catholic!"

He looked at me, distressed. "They have to be!" he said. "All my family is Catholic, every single one of them. And," he paused, avoiding my gaze, "we have to baptize the baby as soon as possible."

What in the Sam Hill was going on here? I tried to stay calm and think this through. While I wasn't opposed to having our baby baptized (no skin off my nose, I figured), I wasn't so sure about signing our kids up to be Catholics. This needed investigation—pronto.

Soon after, I visited a Catholic church and found out what would be required of us should we baptize our baby, whom we had named Frederick. My husband, Fred, as the Catholic, would be required to take Baby Fred to church, but no such thing was expected of me. Through baptism, my son would be welcomed into the Catholic faith and would be freed from original sin.

This is where the Catholic Church differs significantly from Protestant churches, of course. Both believe that we are born with original sin. In the Catholic Church babies are baptized, however, and their original sin is taken away. In Protestantism, contrastingly, the belief is that when you reach the age of maturity and can consciously recognize the meaning of the baptismal act, you must be born a second time—"born again"—into a willing repentance of sin, entering into a new life through Christ.

These different understandings of baptism didn't bother me then and don't bother me today. I have known far too many real believers in both my family and my husband's to ever think that this difference in theology is important when it comes to having a passion for Christ. What *is* of supreme importance when you are a believer is the *personal* relationship with Christ, which takes commitment. Your church attendance is your outward expression of your faith, and it is important because Jesus himself ordained that his followers must worship together. But your personal relationship—your one-on-one connection with Christ—is what will carry you through the peaks and valleys of your life and allow you to experience the real joys and miracles of authentic faith.

Think if it this way: In the classic old movie *The Wizard of Oz*, the first scenes of the movie, before the main character, Dorothy, arrives in the fictional place called Oz, are presented in black and white. But when Dorothy first sees that magical land of Oz, the movie then switches to vibrant color; every color imaginable seems to be splashed on the screen. Now consider this: what if that whole movie had been shot in black and white? It would have technically been the same movie, but it wouldn't have offered nearly the same experience.

The same is true with faith. A *personal* relationship with Christ turns on the color. Church attendance alone, even if accompanied by the other things you are "supposed to do" as a follower of Christ, keeps your faith in black and white. And what a shame that would be! The truth for anyone searching is just this simple (although it is often presented in a much more complicated way): Jesus offers life forever with him and is waiting to be your friend. Think about that for a moment: *Jesus is waiting to be your friend.*

I often remember an experience I had when our first beloved baby was a little older; I was visiting a church in Rehoboth Beach, Delaware, where our family was vacationing. I had gone to the cry room with Baby Fred, not wanting his cries to disturb the worshippers in the main church.

There was a toddler in the cry room with us, an adorable little boy about three years old, dressed in a cute coordinating outfit and bright red sneakers. He wore a protective helmet on his head and moved like the wind around the room, unable to settle on a toy. It was clear that the little boy had some sort of developmental disorder, and as I sat down on the floor and tucked Baby Fred's blankets around him in his carrier, I said a quick prayer for the boy.

Suddenly, that little boy ran to me and began hitting me over the head with his little fists, then grabbed at handfuls of my hair. Surprised and shocked, I ducked my head under my arms and yelped, while angling my body over Baby Fred's to keep him safe. The toddler's mother was on him in a shot, tucking his arms to his side and whispering urgently to him, *Jesus is our friend. Jesus is our friend. Come to us now, Baby Jesus.*

The little boy went limp, allowing his mother, who was apologizing profusely, to bring him to the other side of the room. My heart ached for the mother and her beautiful son who seemed trapped inside a deep well of mental and physical frustration.

Today when I think back to that event, I wonder how many of us, believers and non-believers, have our own impairment of a spiritual nature to deal with— running from thing to thing, idea to idea, to capture our interest or soothe our pain. Perhaps we just need someone whispering *Jesus is your friend* to help us make sense of this life, and the heartbreak and confusion it often doles out to us.

It was a truly joyous day for Fred and me as parents when Baby Fred was baptized. I felt a surge of love and pride as the priest gently poured water over his head, welcoming him into a global family of believers, in the name of the Father, the Son, and the Holy Spirit—that blessed Trinity. The happiness both of our families felt was indeed special.

Beginning around this time, a question presented itself with more and more persistence. I was a mother now, responsible for someone else's life, both physical and spiritual.

What did I really believe? I still didn't know. I was making all the right moves outwardly in regards to faith, but inside, I had substantial doubts. Much of the time I was pretending. I was developing only an intellectual understanding of God and Jesus. Did I have anything more?

Takeaway for the Searcher
What is much more important than which Christian denomination you join is a willingness to open yourself up to a personal relationship with Christ. Then, find a Bible-based church that feels right for you.

Takeaway for the Christian
Emphasize a new believer's growth in their personal relationship with Christ rather than what church they choose; church attendance alone will not provide the lasting foundation that will see the new believer through the ups and downs of life.

CHAPTER 7

The Mighty Wind

Irish playwright and poet George Bernard Shaw once said, "The fact that a believer is happier than a skeptic is no more to the point than the fact that a drunken man is happier than a sober one." Back when I was a teenager, I could definitely see his point. I often wondered what was making the believers I knew so happy and so certain of a heaven—and a hell—no matter what life threw at them. I wondered if they weren't a bit delusional, despite their happiness. Later in my life, I watched my parents and my new in-laws turn to God with a peaceful confidence, certain their prayers were being heard.

As a girl I had once seen my grandmother down in Florida pray over my grandfather as he lay on the rug after a sudden medical emergency. She was ready to let him go, ready to release him to her God, if that was what the Lord wanted. How in the world did she do that? I knew how much she loved and needed my grandfather. What if there were nothing on the other side?

Children, I'm convinced, are naturally drawn to God, unencumbered by the roadblocks teens and adults throw up at almost every stage of a spiritual journey. At age ten, influenced by the committed faith of my grandparents, I erected a simple altar, made of two cinder blocks and a plank of wood, inside my bedroom closet. I could crawl inside, close the doors, and be alone with my thoughts, trying to form prayers. (I was a closeted Christian—literally!) My altar had a candle and a Bible that my grandmother had gifted me with on my tenth birthday. My parents, although not actively worshipping at the time, supported this endeavor (although they warned me several times about burning the house down with the candle and forbid me to light it).

I sat in there with my clothes on hangers dangling over my head trying to pray and wondering, there in the darkness, about the nature of God. I had had exposure to him from my grandparents and wondered how these people I trusted, whose intellect I respected, believed in this "Creator," this invisible being. My prayers were fumbling, but I look back on the little closet altar with affection. It was my attempt at reaching out to God with little understanding or guidance regarding who he was.

What would cause this, other than the fact that a human longing is within us because there actually is a real, outside presence that will answer it? I received nothing in return from my little closet—no messages from above, no spirits beckoning to me invitingly—and I soon abandoned my tiny space of worship and reflection. But something was calling to me, and in a fumbling, childish way, I was trying to answer that call.

When I was fifteen, a television mini-series aired called *Jesus of Nazareth*. Everyone I knew watched it. (Back then there weren't a million television channels, so new programming was consumed with passion!) The actor who played Jesus, Robert Powell, had an ethereal, almost supernatural quality and presented a supremely compelling "Jesus."

My friends and I watched the program avidly. Was Jesus really as good-looking as this fictional Jesus, with long hair, deep blue eyes, and a gaze that could pierce your soul? Why didn't everyone in the story accept that he was God's Son, even after he performed miracles right before their very eyes? Why was everyone so afraid of him? This mini-series caused me to have lingering questions about Christ and his mission.

I realized as a teen that whether you believe it or not, the whole story of Jesus's birth, life, and death is amazing—full of adventures, heartbreaks, and victories, containing both grave sin and glorious redemption. Even today I am amazed when people say Christianity is "boring" —it really is the greatest, most amazing, most adventurous story ever told, whether you buy into it or not.

However, I was filled with ambivalence for much of my life growing up. And I was hanging on to my questions and doubts even years later, as a new mother. To me, secular life was a dazzling blanket of opportunities laid out before me, mine for the taking, if I worked hard enough and smartly positioned myself for success in marriage, parenting, and my professional life. I often felt impatient with stories of long-suffering Christians. I didn't understand those who "turned the other cheek" under life's harsh or unfair treatment. I had heard plenty of examples after my parents returned to church and were actively engaging with other believers.

They knew people facing serious illness who still felt joyous. They knew people who suffered devastating career setbacks or sudden deaths of loved ones, yet who found even deeper levels to their faith. It sometimes seemed the worse things got, the more these followers trusted, when the opposite course of action obviously would have been more rational. How could they go through trials and still keep believing in a God that allowed them to happen in the first place?

I was visiting my family down in Maryland the summer after our first baby was born, and my mother encouraged me to take a little time for myself by grabbing a towel and heading down to the neighborhood pool. I gratefully accepted—I loved our neighborhood pool, having spent happy summers there growing up, swimming with my friends and lying out in the sun on a beach towel for hours each day. And, new moms don't get much time to themselves, so it's not too smart to turn down a solid offer of childcare for a few hours!

I have always loved my mother's books. I love them because they are hers. I know her eyes have perused the pages; I know her sharp mind has considered the words. I also particularly love that she has always made notes in her margins—I have learned a lot from her annotations on many different topics. Her marginal notes are, to me, a precious window into her thoughts about what is presented in the text. For my time at the pool, I decided to read one of the books I had seen around our home growing up, a yellowed, dog-eared copy of *Mere Christianity* by C. S. Lewis.

I went to the hillside I used to lie on growing up and settled on my towel. I stared up at the broad, leafy trees that had been just saplings back in my childhood but were now providing cool shade. I opened the pages of *Mere Christianity* and began reading. The author, C. S. Lewis, had been a foremost Christian theologian, medieval literature professor, and prolific writer, and I had to concentrate to understand each sentence (it flitted through my mind that a *People* magazine or a light summer beach read might have been more relaxing for an afternoon at the pool than this book!).

One passage struck me, and I read it again and again, my finger tracing the words on the yellowed page. Lewis was describing Jesus, writing: "A man who was merely a man and said the sort of things Jesus said would not be a great moral teacher. He would either be a lunatic—on the level with the man who says he is a poached egg—or else he would be the Devil of Hell. You must make your choice."[2]

I sat up on my towel, thinking furiously. Jesus said that he *literally* was the Son of God, and he was neither a lunatic nor the devil. I also couldn't think of another religion in which the object of human worship claimed, in effect, to *be* God.

I looked at the sun-dappled water in my old neighborhood swimming pool and listened to the sounds around me: birds chirping, the *gulp, gulp* of the pool water lapping the drains, and the murmurs and tinkling laughter of the teenage lifeguards nearby. I hugged my knees and put my head on them, breathing deeply. . .This was making too much sense, I thought. It would have been easier to bring that *People* magazine! I pondered the words of C. S. Lewis in the silence of my heart for months afterward, turning them over and over again, looking for a weakness.

Some time later, we moved from Massachusetts to Connecticut, where we set up our little home in the town of Enfield. Our second son was born, a beautiful baby we named Matthew, and we reveled in his arrival, staring for hours at his blue eyes just like my dad's and his tiny perfect fingers and toes. Nothing speaks to the reality of miracles like the birth of a baby.

In just under three years we had already moved twice for Fred's work, first from Maryland to Massachusetts (close to his family), and then from Massachusetts to Connecticut. Fred was soon traveling most of the week for his sales job, working in New York City three days a week, and I held down the fort at home, which was sometimes lonely and challenging. My parents had recently moved to Geneva, Switzerland, for my father's work, and I missed them terribly also.

One particular morning I sat at our old kitchen table, my head in my hands. Money was tight, and I wasn't sure how I was going to buy everything required for the week—groceries and diapers, plus I needed a small birthday gift for one of my close friends. Fred and I had had a serious discussion about our family budget (or lack thereof) on the phone the night before. Adding further to my stress level, Little Fred, just over three years old, was just finding his voice, so to say, and was busy and talkative from sun-up to sundown. Baby Matt had been up all night with a bad cough, and so I hadn't gotten any sleep in the last twenty-four hours. The kitchen was littered with dishes and pots and pans from dinner the night before, and the trash can in the corner was full of dirty diapers.

I felt a powerful surge of despair and failure and a sudden, crushing doubt about all the choices I had made thus far in my married life. Should I have even gotten married? Were we having children too quickly? Had it been the right decision to move again? Were we really a mess doomed for failure and just couldn't see it?

I wasn't yet a person who regularly prayed, but as tears formed in my eyes, I uttered this prayer. "God, if you are up there," I said aloud, "I need some sign, some proof that you care about me, and that things will improve, and that we're on the right track here. Thank you, God. Amen."

"Pitiful," I thought, my eyes burning with exhaustion. "I don't even believe my own prayer."

But just then, right at the very instant I was completely dismissing my own prayer, I heard a great roaring sound behind me, coming from the direction of my backyard. I stood up and walked over to my kitchen window, amazed. Such a great wind had struck up that the giant trees in my backyard were bending to the left, branches and leaves flying everywhere. The wind could be described only as mighty. I suddenly knew all the way down to my bones that God had created that wind and was answering me—instantly, and with great force. The message that popped into my mind was, *I am here.* As chills ran up my back, I craned my neck to see my neighbor's backyard. Every tree was still. The windstorm was happening only in my yard—for *me.* God knew what I needed in the moment and answered me with an awesome show of power and beauty, using a thing I loved—nature.

I pondered the event, which took place in under a minute, for days afterward. Later, as Little Fred and I picked up sticks and branches from my private windstorm (all other yards around ours were free of debris), I knew with certainty: the Creator of the universe had just spoken to me individually.

Takeaway for the Searcher

God is real and is listening to you, even if you can't feel it. Although I had reached out to him before, he hadn't revealed himself in a custom-tailored way I could relate to until the windstorm. But he had always been there.

Takeaway for the Christian

Keep encouraging any present-day searchers you may encounter as they wait for their own windstorm, reminding them that they are eternally important to God. Providing a good book like *Mere Christianity* may be a way to help someone believe in a God who cares and is real.

CHAPTER 8

The Accident

After the windstorm incident, our little family continued to grow and thrive in Connecticut. I raised our two
adorable, energetic little boys while Fred continued to
work hard as a sales rep, opening up new territories and ex-
panding his skills and knowledge of the paper industry. Life
generally hummed along. . . until one day, it didn't. My grandmother Treva (the same one who had, years before, introduced
me to Jesus) passed away after battling Parkinson's disease. The
boys were about six and nine years old, respectively, and my
mother-in-law, Joanne, came to stay with them so Fred and I
could fly down to North Carolina to celebrate Treva's life and
mourn her passing with my family.

On the plane ride down I was troubled. All those years ago my
grandmother had told me about Christ. Then I had experienced
my windstorm. Still, I rode the spiritual fence, while claiming to
be a believer. Was I a stubborn fraud? Was this "Sunday faith"
enough? It sure didn't feel like it. I knew many, many Christians,
and they didn't need any great personal revelation to call their
faith authentic. They believed because their parents and their
parents before them believed. Their faith was steadfast and
beautiful in its own way, to me. My questioning nature just might
have been preventing me from ever settling down and just wor-

shipping God with true confidence. Not that I didn't worship—I could be moved to tears in both a Catholic Mass and a Baptist service, and I believed God was up there and was watching over me. But it wasn't a sustained, everyday faith; it was a when-I-can-fit-it-in, when-I-think-of-it kind of faith.

We buried my grandmother, and I was struck again by my family's simple yet deep well of belief. They talked about Jesus so normally—as if he lived right down the block instead of somewhere tucked away in the vast universe. It was not uncommon for a relative to sip on some iced tea while saying, "Well, I just thought about the time Jesus went into the desert and prayed, and I knew what to do," or, "Jesus spoke to me right in the moment, and I was so grateful!" Other family members would nod and murmur in assent, the experience a familiar one. How I envied them their connection and their certainty!

After the funeral, Fred and I returned home. Several days later I watched in shock with the rest of the nation as former NFL football player O. J. Simpson was acquitted of the double murder of his ex-wife, Nicole Brown Simpson, and her friend Ron Goldman. On the telephone with Fred, who was working in Rhode Island, I said, "This is the worst thing that could happen today."

But it wasn't—not nearly. A few hours later I asked the boys to go jump in our car; we were out of milk, and I wanted to run down to the local gas station to buy a gallon. As we headed out the door, I paused. I had been wearing one of the few items of my grandmother's that I had been given after her death, a long, multi-jeweled pin. A piece of inexpensive costume jewelry, the pin nevertheless was precious to me because it had been hers. I had nervously played with it, attached to my blouse, as I watched the O. J. verdict.

Now, as we continued to head out the door, I felt something draw me to our small kitchen table, littered with coloring books, homework, and red and blue Legos. "Take the pin off," I felt, rather than heard. The message was clear and insistent: "take the pin off." Shaking my head, I unclasped the pin from my blouse, depositing it among the children's colorful debris.

The boys jumped into the car in their bare feet. Matt sat up front with me; I remember he was contentedly humming a popular song as we drove down Hazard Avenue to get the milk. Fred, behind him in the back seat of the passenger side, was talking about his homework.

We picked up the milk at the gas station, chatting away to one another as we got back into our car. As I started the engine, I noticed it faltered. I decided to go by a friend's house to ask her husband to jump the battery, as it had been giving me trouble lately. My friend's husband happily obliged and recommended that I drive the car around the block to make sure the "jump" had worked.

Back out on Hazard Avenue the three of us in my little family went, talking and laughing together. I suddenly spied a large pick-up truck coming towards us. It had veered over into our lane, but it seemed as though there would have been plenty of time for the driver to correct and move back over. Suddenly, the truck sped up, still in our lane, heading straight for us.

"What is that guy doing?!" I stammered, leaning forward to squint through our windshield, as if that would offer answers. The truck was still not moving over, and its speed was increasing. I checked to my right and to my left; if the truck didn't move over, I would simply move left into his lane—risky, with kids in the car, but doable. On my right, a gulley, woods, and telephone poles prevented me from choosing that direction as an option should I have needed to move out of my lane.

Suddenly, in a burst of speed, the truck was right in front of us, its grill looming in my line of vision. I couldn't move into the other lane, I saw—a third car was already in it, beeping frantically to try and get the truck driver's attention. I was in a sudden crisis. I decided in a split second, before the car hit us, to turn the steering wheel to the right, hoping there would be no impact to the side of the car the boys were on, and that we would also somehow escape bouncing into the gulley.

But that hope was futile. The truck hit us anyway, and the impact was brutal. I saw Matt flying towards our windshield, blonde hair like a halo around his head, before the seat belt snapped him back into his seat. Fred screamed in the back seat as he was thrown forward, and I felt the steering wheel push into my chest and heard my car's left front-end crumple in a moan of twisted metal.

Soon the scene was chaos. The boys were screaming, cars pulled over all around us, eager to help, and red and blue lights swirled in my line of vision as I tried to stay alert. Miraculously, aside from a few scrapes the boys were fine, as was the other driver. I asked emergency personnel over and over again to prove to me that the boys were indeed unhurt, as police held back traffic and firemen tried to rescue me from my vehicle, eventually employing the Jaws of Life to free me. A kind stranger sat behind me in the back seat of my car, making sure I stayed conscious.

It turned out we had narrowly escaped tragedy. We had been hit by a driver who was believed to have been under the influence of drugs and alcohol, although that was never proven. I was in the hospital for a week with broken ribs, a collapsed lung, and scrapes and bruises, but the boys were fine, and that's all that mattered to me.

Lying in my hospital bed, I had many hours to think about what had happened and about the fragility of life. I thought about my sons and my husband and how much I loved them.

And I thought about that pin. I had had the distinct feeling that I was told to take it off as I had left the house. Before I was discharged from the hospital, I met with the doctor who had been caring for me, and I told him about that pin. He asked me to show him where I had worn it, and I pointed to my chest, on the left side.

He nodded somberly. "That pin would have killed you, if you had kept it on; it would have gone right through your heart," he said.

I already knew that. I had been instructed by heaven to remove it. Thank God I listened.

We often turn to God and grow our faith in him during tragedies and then, after the emergency resolves itself, feel guilty when that closeness fades. Why, we think, can't we hang on to that feeling that there is a loving Creator in charge of our fates?

In the moments after the tragic events of September 11, 2001, I happened to be right next-door to my church, at a gymnastics class with our third son, James. As the news became more and more grim, I sought solace in the church building, which was mostly empty.

I knelt down in the pew, little James kneeling beside me, and I noticed some construction workers at the front of the church, also kneeling together. I knew they had been working on the building I had just been in, the gymnastics studio, because I had heard their laughter and their "colorful" language as they had yelled directions to one another, toting long beams on their shoulders. Now, these men were on their knees in their dusty clothes, with their tool belts and work boots on, praying to God for immediate help and mercy for strangers and for our country. I was connected to these workers even though I did not know them; my prayers were the same as theirs.

As they passed us to leave, their expressions somber, one of the men reached out and ruffled James's hair. This workman smiled grimly at me and said in his thick Boston accent, "I wonder if the man upstairs even recognizes my voice, it's been so long." He kept walking.

As the coming days brought more and more heartbreak, I often went to the chapel in another church nearby. I was moved by young businessmen in their suits and ties coming on their lunch hours to pray. The nation experienced record-breaking church attendance after 9/11, as we all sought answers and relief from our grief and looked for some meaning to the pain and loss.

I believe God always welcomes us when we return to communication with him, and he never adopts an attitude of *"Well, finally! What took you so long?!"* He is just glad to see us. And yes, he wants us to continue to love and know him, even after emergencies fade. But as a God of complete justice, he also knows the pressures of modern life and the things that tear us away from faith. That is why I think it must be all the much sweeter to him when we do settle down and focus on loving and getting to know him, cutting through the mess of this cynical, often frightening, fractured age.

Takeaway for the Searcher

God is there in your deepest troubles, danger, and despair. He will make all situations right, and his angels will protect you and guide you. While God never causes tragedy, many Christians have come to faith after a traumatic experience he has used to draw them to him, making something good come from the ashes.

Takeaway for the Christian

God never abandons us, and we will find the answers to life's tragedies on the other side of the veil. Our job is to be there for one another during trying times and to remember how frightening these times are for those with no faith.

CHAPTER 9

Doubts After the Fall

W e moved yet again when Fred and Matt were ten and seven, respectively, traveling back to Massachusetts, this time settling right outside Boston in a comfortable, leafy suburb just north of the city. (This was three years before our third and last child James, our "surprise baby," would arrive.) My across-the-street neighbor, Louise, was a wonderful person. We would sometimes attend her Lutheran church together (I was by that time a baptized Catholic, attending our local Catholic church with my family), and we participated together in a program that began in the Church of England, called Alpha.

Louise was as faithful a person as one could imagine, even under the harshest of circumstances. I learned that after nursing her husband until he died of cancer, Louise brought her mother into their home and nursed her, too, through a long and frustrating journey with dementia. Although Louise would care for, pray with, and sing to her mother, Louise also endured times when her mother, because of her disease, would accuse Louise of awful things, including trying to poison her food. Yet any daily frustrations Louise had were always followed by her expression of how blessed she was—her mother was still alive, her own health was good, and she had dear neighbors, extended family, and friends.

Life was always good, in Louise's final analysis. Louise remained faithful through it all and has to this day a quality of innocence and simple joy in being alive that I so admire. And, she has a laugh that can delight even the crankiest of souls!

One day Louise's brother, who had just retired and was looking forward to lots of time with his grandkids, came over to trim a few of the fir trees on Louise's property. Although she asked him not to bother, he good-naturedly insisted, wanting to clear away some of the tangled lower branches. The plan was that he would do this quick yard chore and then enjoy lunch with Louise and their mother. Since my home was right across the street, I had a clear view of Louise's property from my front windows. but I was working on my computer in the back of the house during her brother's visit and didn't see any of the activity in her yard.

Louise, worried about her brother being up on a ladder, went outside after making sure her mother was comfortable indoors. She held the bottom of the ladder for him as he reached for branches with a power saw. She occasionally looked back to the window where she could check to see her mother's silhouette. Louise watched her brother work while praying this prayer: "Lord, please keep him safe."

Well, her brother reached too far while cutting some limbs over his head, and one side of the ladder suddenly pivoted away from the tree with an immense force. The ladder swayed backwards and, with Louise powerless to stop it, fell to the ground, throwing Louise's brother off it and into our street. He sustained a massive head injury and died just hours later. Not only did Louise have to witness that horror, but she had to call the ambulance while her brother lay dying in the road—and then she had to go inside and tell her mother that her son was dead.

When Louise called me after the ambulance had left and told me what had happened, I was shocked. My heart broke that my dear friend, then in her seventies, had to go through this devastating experience. I felt anguish that I had not known about her emergency in our street; I could have sat with her in the road as she waited for the ambulance with her brother bleeding beside her. And I was slayed to learn that Louise, faithful despite whatever life had previously thrown at her, had actually been asking God for her sibling's safety before he fell.

My own faith was shaken. How could God not see Louise's goodness and respect her wish? While Louise seemed to move from grief to acceptance through constant prayer, I resisted such a reaction. Could God really care at all, if he would allow this to happen to such a true, virtuous woman?

Finally, I one day asked my friend how she did it, how she stayed in communion with God after he turned away from her prayer. Her answer? "Jesus is with me as I go through this. I can actually *feel* it," she told me, as we sat outside in her car after going on a grocery store run together. "And if I'm going *through* this, it means there is another side to it. God never causes bad things to happen, but sometimes bad things just do happen in life. He will make all things work together for good in the end," she said, smiling tiredly. "At times during all this, I have felt Jesus's closeness so personally, it is like he is actually hugging me," she continued. "Don't ask me how I know, because it is a mystery, but I am certain—100 percent—that my brother is just fine now, finer than he's ever been."

But this explanation was not good enough for me. I was not as far down the road faith-wise as Louise was, and I sometimes worried that one horrific personal loss would reveal my faith to be a house of cards, collapsing when tested. To be honest, there are times when I still worry about that. But Louise's response in the face of her loss was also her testimony. I have carried it with me, and it continues to deepen my faith over time.

A few years later, Louise's sister fell ill with a brain tumor, and although Louise had been planning to move out to sunny California to be nearer to her grandkids, she put off her own happiness to nurse her sister until she died. As I visited Louise at her sister's home, I finally understood how Louise had a different view on life's hardships as well as a different idea of why we are here and how we are to face life's trials. From that point forward, I began to be a better friend and a better person, I believe. Strangely enough, I was with Louise at the moments that both her mother and her sister took their last breaths. Although I had missed being there at the death of her brother, I was grateful that God made it possible for me to actively support Louise at the moment her other loved ones died. We were able to say prayers together and to quietly marvel about the moment this earthly life ends and eternity begins.

Louise helped me to understand that while life is often excruciatingly painful and finite, we are not alone. Her experiences also showed me that we must accept the fact that much of life on this side of heaven is a mystery. As I was gaining some clarity about that, a powerful concept was also beginning to form in my mind: could it be that this life is not about happiness, but meaning?

I recalled the people I would see in my parents' church back when I was a teen. They endured divorces, children going down wrong or dangerous paths, sudden and tragic deaths of loved ones, and many more terrible situations in life. But like the Whos from Whoville in the old children's classic *The Grinch Who Stole Christmas*, they kept celebrating life, even in the face of trouble. Why? Because these people, like Louise, had a joy in their hearts that couldn't be taken away. Life events were like waves, and their faith was like a rock that would not break no matter how many assaults it took. These Christians also seemed to have more capacity for laughter—good, honest laughter, not at anyone else's expense—than more cynical folks I knew.

I seemed to be learning through these Christian people that meaning and service are the goals of this life. After all, many lives, sadly, are short. I remembered that when I was trapped alone in my car after my accident, I did have peace knowing that my children were safe, even if I should die. My life hadn't been long, I figured, but it had meant something—I had brought some wonderful boys into this world. If this were all true, and there were a heaven and a purpose and a coming glory I could not even imagine, my thought started to be, "Sign me up!"

Takeaway for the Searcher

There will be people whom God puts in your path for you to learn from, your "Louises." Keep your eyes open for them; they can change your life and teach you about his true nature.

Takeaway for the Christian

God may position you to be someone else's "Louise"; take it seriously and execute your role honestly and joyfully. Your efforts and example may lead someone to faith.

CHAPTER 10

Why Have I Not Heard of This God?

I mentioned earlier that I was baptized in the Catholic faith—just a few months after my second baby, Matthew, was baptized. What a momentous day! As my priest and close friend Father Francis Kerwan of Holy Family Catholic Church in Enfield, Connecticut, poured water over my head, my husband's parents standing by my side as my chosen godparents, I knew my life had changed. I had participated in months of formal study prior to this big day, and my decision to join the Catholic Church was the right one for me at that time.

I, like many people who join a denomination as an adult, am very open and flexible to all expressions of worship within the Christian faith, as long as they are scripturally based. I feel just as at-home in a Baptist or Lutheran church as I do in a Catholic church. I enjoy the exchange of ideas among the different "branches" of the faith, as well as with people of no faith. Today, I feel that the most important things are that we live our faith, defend it when necessary, and progress in our personal journey toward God.

Yet there were things about the Catholic Church, specifically its vast wealth and the veneration of Mary, which I had been hesitant about. Father Kerwan, however, said something during one of our lessons that had clinched my decision: "You can argue different points about every type of church for the rest of your life, Deirdre. . . Or, you can start to actively worship with your family and others in community with Jesus Christ."

This made sense to me; people have arguments and concerns within their church, but they show up, they commit to worshipping together, and they keep Christ at their center. I also seemed to feel God's pleasure at the idea of our growing family in the pews together as one, and doors within my heart and mind seemed to open somewhat with each lesson I was receiving in Father Kerwan's comfortable office. How many times I stared at the crucifix on his wall, Jesus hanging above me on the cross, as I pondered my own future. But I still did not know Christ personally. I was still pretending.

Ten years later, our third baby boy James was also baptized. I felt we were trying to do everything necessary to bring up our three sons to know and love Jesus Christ. If they could learn that from us, we figured, we would be giving them the best gift a parent possibly could. . . Now, a quick note for parents—easier said than done, that "spiritual parenting." God creates each child with his own free will and then calls to them individually. The truth is, many believers have children raised in the faith who wander away, questioning all they have learned, trying out other ideas as to what the true purpose of life is. I think that is fine and even expected. The parent can pray for them, support them, and love them no matter what, while still freely expressing their own Christian faith. You can't make someone accept Christ; what would be the point of that?

In the same way we wouldn't want our children to *have* to love us, God doesn't want us to have to love him. I believe that God, who created us and knows our nature better than we know it ourselves, invites our questions, our doubts, and our confusion. I have since grown to learn that he can handle it; he is the Creator of the whole universe! He wants us to go through our process and come to him willingly; more than anything, I think, he wants even just a fledgling relationship with us during the journey—which is what this little book is all about.

Anyway, in an effort to make sure my children were at least educated in their faith, so they could eventually profess their commitment genuinely, I began teaching the Catholic version of Sunday School, CCD (Confraternity of Christian Doctrine), starting when they were very young. It was a unique experience teaching my own kids—and they weren't necessarily thrilled about having their mom for a teacher. (Note: kids act out more when their parent is their teacher; trust me on that!)

It is important to realize here that although I was teaching CCD every week and instructing children on their faith, my own faith was still in a place of confusion and extremely rudimentary. I was operating from a sense of obligation and a wish to see my children raised properly, not out of any true acceptance. Although I had had several amazing moments during my lifetime when I could feel God's presence (most notably my windstorm), I still didn't have a personal understanding of Christ, not yet. I understood *intellectually* and respected that Jesus was God's own son, but I didn't feel he was essential to my belief in God. I also didn't understand how his sacrifice had served humanity. *How* had he taken all our sins upon himself—and *why*, after the way human beings had treated him?

Over the years, busy with raising children, running a home, and working part-time as a freelance writer and columnist, I had prayed when I could for understanding about Jesus—but further exploration into his nature definitely wasn't at the top of my to-do list.

One afternoon I pulled up into our driveway with my oldest son, Fred, now 14, who was slumped in the passenger seat. He was grousing about CCD, and how he didn't like it; it was a waste of his time, it was dumb, and he didn't want to attend anymore. I looked at his face, an angry frown growing there. Underneath his grumblings I heard real frustration: "what in the world does this have to do with my life?" he was saying.

I myself grew frustrated trying to explain yet again why it was important to get a basic education in faith. I could explain for the one-millionth time how God loved him, and that faith would carry him through dark times in his life, and that eternity was a long time—and I'd like him to be there to enjoy it! I knew it sounded like *blah blah blah* to him.

Suddenly, I found the words. "Fred, when you are at the top of the mountain, your snowboard tipping downhill, and you're looking forward to barreling down as fast as you can, God is there with you, at the very center of that moment. He wants you to feel that exhilaration—that rush—when you enjoy his creation. When you jump off the diving board or go body-surfing, he is there," I continued. "When you play your guitar, he is there, enjoying what you enjoy, in it with you. God isn't just a God of rules; he is a God of adventure, and wonder, and nature, and he is rooting for you. In fact, he created in you the part that loves the outdoors and loves jumping, diving, snowboarding, running. That is the God I want you to learn about."

Fred stared at me, wide-eyed. "Why have I not heard of this God?" he asked me, his whole being appearing to calm down. I was touched by his sincere, almost old-timey expression of surprise. My mind seemed to calm down too as I sat with my son and considered what we had just said.

I had focused so much on the rules, and was so consumed with teaching all about being a "good Christian," that I often forgot that God created nature so we could enjoy it; he is a lively and interested God, deeply involved in all aspects of our lives and our deepest longings. Indeed, he created some of us to be adventurous—to explore and discover, to climb mountains and plumb the depths of the ocean. Remember I mentioned that nature is a good indicator of the Spirit of God? Well, *our* natures are also a good indicator of God's spirit. Fulfilling the destiny—the one that God already has mapped out for us, if we are in total compliance with his will—may include jumping off waterfalls, exploring caves, or diving out of airplanes.

If the adventure is blessed by God, it is one you should take. The Bible, God's living Word, is chock full of adventures. As you begin to familiarize yourself with it, you will be amazed at the daring, courage, and physical tests contained in the greatest story ever told. Perhaps with children we focus too much on the rules of the Bible and don't give enough time to its hearty adventure or recognize our own adventure stories which a loving God himself has built into our lives. Standing at the top of a mountain you've climbed to watch the sunrise, or scuba diving in the ocean with fish of every size and color, or trekking through the desert marveling at its reptiles and native plants aplenty, or skiing as fast as you can down a wooded and starkly beautiful mountain trail—all are gifts from God. We must not think of God as lurking and waiting only in our churches; he is everywhere, in every good and decent endeavor. He calls to us with these adventures, perhaps whispering, "I am here, too. I am everywhere. Enjoy the beauty I have created for you!"

Here is part of St. Patrick's "Breastplate" or "Lorica" prayer, in which he affirms nature's power and its tangible, physical gifts to humans:

> I arise today
> Through the strength of heaven:
> Light of sun,
> Radiance of moon,
> Splendor of fire,
> Speed of lightning,
> Swiftness of wind,

Depth of sea,
Stability of earth,
Firmness of rock.[3]

This is God, not only a Creator of commandments and laws but also a God of wonder, adventure, and the natural world, who loves us deeply and is pleased when we enjoy his creation.

Another lesson from my kids comes to mind as well. My second son, Matt, has always had an innate connection to God; he seems to have been born with a "direct line" to heaven. He was a peace-loving, gentle child and has grown into an honorable, happy young man. One day when he was about seven, Matt was helping me with housework. While I swept the floor, he dusted the woodwork in our living room with a cloth, humming as he polished the doorway's moldings.

Suddenly Matt stopped and peered up at me with his bright blue eyes, wide and clear beneath his light blonde bangs. "Mom," he asked, "is it okay if I love God more than I love you?" I smiled, impressed by his question. How did this sweet little boy come up with these deep thoughts?

I answered, "Yes, that is fine! God should be Number One—and I know how much you love me." I stopped sweeping and went over and gave him a hug.

A few moments later Matt said, "Mom, I have another question."

I smiled. "Lay it on me," I said back.

He looked at me again with those big eyes, windows right into his seven-year-old soul, and asked, "Do you love God more than you love me?"

Gulp. From the mouths of babes! I was learning about faith from a little boy, and the lesson seemed to be: genuine, sustaining faith requires us to put the Lord first in *all* things. If we do this, then we can truly experience the most precious of relationships, like the one between mother and child.

Takeaway for the Searcher

God is so many things, not just a rule-maker. He is also compassionate, loving, and encouraging. He seeks our best—including what makes us feel uniquely alive. Children are sometimes the best reminders of all the energizing, authentic facets of God.

Takeaway for the Christian

Are you forgetting about multiple aspects of the divine personality of God? Sometimes we focus on sharing the rules so much that we forget to share that he delights in and approves of adventure, laughter, and fun. This is extremely important for you to show to anyone searching for God!

CHAPTER 11

The Problem of Evil

Perhaps at this point in your life you have allowed that there may be a specific creator of the universe, and that creator sometimes fashions mystical, supernatural experiences like my windstorm to announce his presence and power. You are even pleased to learn that this God not only creates rules for our good, but revels in our laughter, adventures, joys, and happiness.

Great!

Soon enough in your pilgrimage, however, you bump up against the problem of evil—a problem that has confounded everyone, even the faithful, since the beginning of human history.

Why would a loving God allow evil, heartbreak, and tragedy? Can he really love us that much, if he allows unendurable pain even when he could stop it? We have all either heard of, or—sadly—experienced unimaginable evil. A baby is murdered by its own mother. A plane is hijacked and flies into a building, killing thousands. Whole families are swept away by a sudden tsunami as they holiday together. Darkness wins, and our faith, if we have any, is shaken yet again.

The problem of evil is very complicated, and there are many books and essays written on just this topic. Let's try to look at this complex, multi-layered conundrum very briefly but also logically. First, we must realize that evil is the product of sin. Whether or not you use the word "sin" to describe it, the idea remains the same. We can all feel that we possess a level of depravity within us: that dark and devilish thought we can't get rid of, that careless and hurtful action that affected another, that willful decision that changed or, in the direst of cases, perhaps even ruined another's life, or our own. If God stopped evil created by humans, he would also stop our thinking, decision-making, and, most of all, freedom—which we as people crave as a fundamental right. He would step in at each and every instance of wrongdoing and change it to good—which he could—but we would no longer be free. Simplified, imagine if your parents (and God is the ultimate parent) had not allowed you to make even one mistake. They rushed in before you could do the bad or stupid thing and stopped you. Sure, you might have lived a nearly spotless childhood, but you would have hated it, chafing at your constraints and never learning anything.

In the same way, God allows us free will: free will to love him and free will to turn away from him. Free will to do good or free will to do bad. The existence of evil doesn't point towards there being no God; it points instead to a rational, just God. Free will naturally contains the potential for a fair portion of evil; apart from God, humans are capable of great evil. But it is important that we be free to act, and live, and do as we see fit—and God lets us. That whole process includes evil acts by people. We just can't have it both ways (free will and perfection on earth).

But what about natural tragedies that people have no hand in, like earthquakes? Wouldn't it be easy for an all-powerful God to stop this devastation and pain, to unwind the tornado or calm a deadly sea? "We know that the whole creation has been groaning as in the pains of childbirth right up to the present time," says the Bible, directly speaking to suffering (Rom. 8:22).

Here's the problem: our world is *fallen*. (Uh-oh, there's one of those "churchy" terms!) The Bible says that when the first man and woman fell into sin (when Eve forgot God's instructions and was tempted by the serpent, and then she and Adam ate that cursed apple), nature became cursed, too. Sinful humans could no longer live in a perfect paradise, so nature itself was affected by their sin. (Note: Some Christians have a strict, literal interpretation of the stories in the Bible, like this one, Noah's Ark, or Jonah and the whale, while others think the stories are merely metaphors meant to explain Biblical concepts. While I am in the first camp, I have no problem with the second. As long as the concept is from God and the Bible, I'm good. On the other hand, I of course don't know for sure whether God created the world in seven days or if it was more of a "Big Bang" situation, and I'm fine with not knowing. I'm just glad to be here!)

Throughout history, as seen in the Bible, God uses natural disasters such as plagues to interact with humans. These cataclysms teach us that life is fragile and time is infinitely precious. In how many instances have we heard a survivor of a tragedy say that this is exactly what they learned? And of course, since God sees all of space and time at once, he can save people from tragedies; or, if he doesn't save someone's life, he can take that death and work it for good in others' lives, because he is all-powerful. That victim, we hope, is with God in Paradise, free forever from all worldly cares.

But for those of us still here on earth, we are "east of Eden," like the dispossessed Adam and Eve, according to the Bible. And it is a battleground full of choice and opportunity. Through our own strivings, we can try to be decent and moral. But even through non-stop good works, we cannot regain Paradise on earth. (Even the most resolute pro-humanist atheist will probably admit that the world can never be made perfect by us.) The Bible story of Adam, Eve, and the apple, in summary, teaches us that we must listen to God because he wants only our good, and we should trust him and his word in all things—not an easy thing for humans with that all-important free will to follow!

Now, as for the excuse for evil some use, best captured in that old phrase "the devil made me do it". . . I believe that the devil does exist; he is a literal dark power that seeks to destroy our hearts, bodies, minds, and souls, and he does it with relish. But I also believe that we as humans have a crucial responsibility to refrain from evil acts, both large and small. We have our own will, and God made that will free: to love him or not; to do good in our time on earth, or not. To blame the devil is to shirk our own role in the darkness that is a large part of the human experience.

So, does God really care that we are going through this exposure to evil, to temptation? Is he just waiting around, watching to see if we mess up? No. Just because God allows evil in this world, this doesn't mean he has a "hey, humans, good luck with all that!" mentality. That aloof perspective just wouldn't make sense if God loves us so deeply and is indeed intimately involved in our lives. What would be the purpose of him allowing us to stay in our fallen state alone?

We have a pet tortoise named Gary. He is an unusual pet, and he has provided hours of laughs, entertainment, and unique party conversations, to be sure! We welcomed Gary into the family about fifteen years ago, and he is approximately twenty years old. And since tortoises can live to be one hundred or even beyond, Gary is a mere adolescent in the tortoise lifecycle. In warmer months, we allow Gary to "free-range" around the bottom floor of our house, leaving his crate and going wherever he wants to go. Gary loves to crawl underneath one of our television cabinets, where he often gets stuck. To enter, his shell fits under only one side of the cabinet, but he never remembers that and struggles to exit by trying the other three sides over and over again. It is quite the sight to see a tortoise, collecting hairballs as he goes, straining to crawl out from under a television stand. It has always baffled me that Gary doesn't remember, no matter how many times I show him, that freedom is possible by accessing that one side only.

Aren't we similar?

So, what did God do for the descendants of his original "children of wrath" (Adam and Eve), who fell away from the joy he had planned? He performed a holy action, one that resonates mightily down through the ages as we continue struggling today, compulsively and obsessively trying to crawl out from under the things holding us captive. And what is that action?

He sent Jesus.

Takeaway for the Searcher

The problem of evil is complex. God allows us free will, which also permits horrific, human-contrived evil into our world. He does not stand idly by, however—he will intervene in tragedy or work it into something good. He sent a solution to our fallen state, his son Jesus.

Takeaway for the Christian:

Tread carefully around the problem of evil; this is a very hard concept for anyone searching for faith to understand and deserves to be handled candidly, soberly, and with great thought. Every human being, believer or not, grapples with the problems of evil, grief, and pain.

CHAPTER 12

This Life-Changing Christ

A fter I believed in the *personal reality* of Jesus, it was hard for me to ever imagine how I, the "Great Pretender," had taught others about Christianity without a direct, personal knowledge of Christ himself. How had I told children to believe in God's Son, when I only intellectually believed in him as a concept, an idea?

Here is how that changed. It happened all at once, in a moment.

Interestingly, Louise, my neighbor, was present for my life-changing revelation. She and I were driving home together from one of our last Alpha meetings. It was raining very hard, and the windshield wipers on Louise's car rhythmically slapped the glass, clearing the spattering raindrops as we traveled along the slick town roads.

My mind was alert; I had been feeling unusually emotional at Alpha that night, almost on edge. Concepts we were learning about were breaking through, I felt, and I was considering the real possibility of being a better Christian: Doing more. Helping others more. Solidifying my right to be in heaven someday. In other words...I still wasn't getting it! You can't earn heaven; that's what Christ died to give us. But I couldn't feel that until this upcoming moment.

We pulled up in front of my house, and Louise left the car engine idling as we talked—about nothing at all, really. I was staring out the windshield looking into the dark through the pattering raindrops, when a slow, warm feeling spread over me, and I felt, in a sense, suddenly outside myself, outside my conversation with Louise, outside of established space and time. The only way I know how to describe it is that it was like *a dawning*.

"It's all real," I thought, staring out into the rain. Christ does exist, and he is who he said he is! He *is* God's Son, and he lives today—right now. And he died for me. *Me.* I had always been so confused by this notion, but suddenly all I had heard, been told, and exposed to throughout my life clicked into place, like a key in a lock. Jesus had taken onto himself all the sins of humanity—current, past, and future—and loaded with sin, sacrificed himself. So, if I had been the only one on earth at the time of his death, he still would have willingly gone through with it so that I might live on after my physical death. It's hard to conceive of, but it is true. If *you* had been the only person on earth, he would have done the same for you. As humans we can't wrap our heads around that kind of sacrificial love, and I think we instinctively, self-denyingly move away from it.

This is the most amazing concept I will ever realize, and I felt the truth of that in the car with Louise, there at the curb in the rain. The enormity of my realization washed over me, and the fundamental change it brought to my life hit me like a sledgehammer. I now believed in Christianity—*really believed!* That Wizard of Oz technicolor had been turned on, and I would never be the same.

I didn't share any of this with Louise but leaned over and hugged her as I said my goodbyes, eager to be alone with my new reality.

I leaped up my front steps and ran inside my darkened house. I strode to a bookshelf in my living room and pulled down a simple collection of children's Bible stories, one I often read to our smallest son James. I smiled through tears. It was if I could finally understand each and every word on the colorful printed pages, standing there in my raincoat and squinting to read by the dim light of the hallway lamp. My mind, my heart, my soul, and my will were all in accord, and all glowing deeply and radiantly, with energy, acknowledgement, and, at long last, comprehension.

It was as if all the snippets of information about Jesus that I had learned throughout my life were now pieces of colorful fabric carefully placed along my own unique timeline. In that moment in the car with Louise, the Holy Spirit gathered all those pieces up and created a beautiful quilt of truth and understanding that I could wrap around me for the rest of my life. My realization felt extremely personal; it was clear in those moments that I was somehow uniquely precious within the vast, incalculable universe.

What was it that had become clear, exactly? Below, I will try my best to sum up my other specific understandings from those first moments:

My past counted in heaven. Although I had discounted my time acting or "pretending," I realized now that I *had* been in at least some sort of relationship with God since I started my journey towards Christ. God had been present and working in my life the whole time, honoring my questions and my doubts and also the fact that I tried to behave like a Christian even though I hadn't bought into Christ as God's Son (in fact, I had rarely even thought about it). Once I did truly believe, however, the "technicolor" had been turned on, leaving the past in black and white.

Christ was not merely a prophet or wise man of his time—he was and is literally God's Son. Remember now what C. S. Lewis so succinctly explained—if Jesus wasn't God's Son, he was a crazy person who claimed to be. And you won't ever hear anyone call Jesus Christ crazy. Christ willingly died for humanity, making him so much more than a moral teacher.

God could have stopped Christ's agonizing death at any time, because God is all-powerful. But Christ's death fulfilled the promises of the Old Testament, writings inspired by God himself, about the arrival of a Messiah. Jesus didn't want to die—his human side asked God to stop it, if it were God's will to do so—but Jesus understood that he was fulfilling sacred prophesy.

In the way that animals were sacrificed to the Lord in the Bible, Jesus was a human sacrifice—loaded down with humanity's sin— that God accepted. What did Christ's crucifixion give us? It created a clear path to heaven, so we can spend eternity in God's presence. Life is all too fleeting, we all know, and eternity beckons to each person, regardless of status, wealth, or physical health. We *will* die. Christ's death wiped away the sin that keeps us from God; Jesus took it all upon himself, even asking God to forgive those who crucified him.

The people of that day were looking for a political king, but Christ came to explain that life is so much more: it is, plain and simple, about love. God watched his Son tortured to death by the very people Jesus had come to save. We are here to love one another and worship one loving Creator, and Jesus tried so hard to tell everyone that.

You cannot earn salvation, a "churchy" word that means the ultimate transformation of a soul that someday rests with God in heaven. We live in a society where we have been trained to earn good things, but Christ's gift is bestowed on us with no strings attached. He paid the price so we don't have to. This doesn't mean good works aren't important; rather, it means that good works will flow from your Christianity as a result of it, not be the cause of it. Remember the hymn I referred to earlier, "Amazing Grace"? The lyrics say it all:

> Amazing grace, How sweet the sound,
> That saved a wretch like me!

> I once was lost, but now am found;
> Was blind, but now I see.

Grace, not works, saves.

Christ is the path to God. We pray "in Jesus's name" because we go to God through Christ; the two cannot be separated out. I was believing in God without believing in his Son—it was like holding and loving a baby doll instead of a real baby. While I intellectually accepted Christ, my heart hadn't ever really welcomed him as crucial to the experience, until that rainy night sitting in a car with a friend. Like my windstorm, I can't explain it, which is the mystery of faith. Believing in God is a stunning supernatural experience.

Takeaway for the Searcher

This type of experience is available to you! I could never have guessed that I would eventually have this type of life-changing experience. Trust that it will happen to you too. Continue your investigations (read the Bible, think, and pray about Christ), and be ready for Christ to reach out to you.

Takeaway for the Christian

Encourage others around you. Even so-called Christians you know may not have a real relationship with Christ; I didn't. It is so easy today to get lazy about our faith. When was the last time you were really *excited* about spending eternity with God and his Son Jesus?

CHAPTER 13

What Now?

You may be wondering what my life looked like and felt like after my revelation. Was my life suddenly charmed and inspirational to others, with wisdom to spare? Did I float around with a beatific smile on my face, extending a hand to all who needed it while becoming a better wife, mother, daughter, sister, and friend?

The answer is a hard "no." In fact, in many ways life got harder. While I reveled in my new understanding, I still felt unworthy—a feeling many believers battle. Maybe this is because we also have a fuller sense of God's glory once we have a personal experience—and in comparison, we humans can look and feel pretty pitiful. We just have to keep telling ourselves that we *are* worthy of God's love, no matter what state we are in. I also felt a lot of temptations come my way, immediately testing my new status as a "real" Christian. I was beset by doubt, too—did I really get the unexpected but needed gift of grace that night in Louise's car, or was it simply a hopeful imagining? Remember, God had visited my backyard, moving sticks and branches around supernaturally in my own personal windstorm, and still I had had doubts. The human capacity for doubt is very strong and always has been, throughout the ages.

We are human, and these are all understandable reactions. The fact is, I did not become a better person, but I became a person who *wanted to be* better. I became someone who felt she had a trusted confidant in Christ, that dearest friend to whom I could safely reveal my messiest, ugliest, weakest self. I also began to pray about my most private hopes and wishes, as well as disappointments and failures—haltingly at first, worried that Christ would somehow say, "Well gosh, I didn't know all *that*. Forget it!" But he hasn't forgotten me. I still marvel that God and his Son would care about my worries and have the mystical capacity to take on not only my cares, but everyone else's, too.

All in all, I still fall short. The truth is, all true believers do. And this is a very important part of being a Christian. No one should wait to become Christian until they "get their act together." I will share some things about myself now that may make you more comfortable about the idea of believing in Christ while having problems (which means you are human).

First, I still can't locate all the books in the Bible. Yep—I am one of those people who still flip around desperately in a lecture or sermon, hoping to land on the right chapter. But I am growing in that, and a Bible study I'm now participating in with close friends helps.

Next, I sometimes watch television shows and movies that are questionable. I can lose an afternoon to edgy murder mysteries or a string of *Dateline* episodes, and that material is dark. But I am a much more discerning viewer now and am still growing in this area, too. I actively seek out quality programming that glorifies Jesus and would be pleasing to him.

In addition, I have some quirks, moods, and traits that many might not consider "Christian." For instance, I don't sit around listening to hymns and sipping tea; I absolutely love rock music, and I enjoy a good glass of wine or two. Also, I can be impatient—ask my husband! I often don't look like the picture of the relaxed Christian who is confident that everything will work out.

God knows this about me, and he knows that I am trying and will doggedly *keep* trying (I'm also stubborn!).

There are many more facets of me, large and small, that I won't bore you with, but they are there, and they may not seem too "Christian." However, they absolutely *do not* disqualify me from relationship with God and Jesus. Imagine if one of your relatives or best friends said to you, "I have decided that your faults and problems are horrifying to me, and I just can't deal with them anymore. You're not good enough for me, honestly. So, this is it—we're through!" Well, God and his Son will *never* say this to you— ever. Period. (Though honestly, sometimes human beings will.) I once had a friend who worried that her smoking kept her from true relationship with God. *Never!* You can bring to him the ugliest, nastiest parts of your character or your past and he will offer you redemption and a way forward. You can lay it out before him, secure that you will not be turned away. Don't focus on the rules. Focus on the relationship.

When you begin your relationship, pray as if you were speaking to a trusted friend. Share the concerns of your heart in whatever way feels comfortable. Tell God you're not even sure he is up there at all, if that's the way you feel. Express your doubts—he can handle it. As you grow in your comfort and trust levels, your prayers will grow in both sincerity and in celebration—you will *want* to tell God, over and over again, how magnificent he is!

I say all of this to lead up to something wonderful. You may be thinking, "So I am supposed to pray to God and Jesus, both of whom I can't see, and trust them with my future? I may even change into a Christian, which sounds scary. Sounds a little pointless. What's in it for me?" . . . So here's the amazing part, what's in it for you: a relationship to top all relationships—a supernatural relationship with God, who loves you more than any person ever could. A bond with Jesus, the best friend you will ever have, who understands what it is like to be human, and who understands what it is like to be heartbroken. Access to the Holy

Spirit, who will make God's messages to you both understandable and actionable. A life-changing understanding of yourself and this world. An ability to find meaning even in the most terrible of situations. The realization that those you hold dear also have the chance at eternity—being with God forever.

Plus, when you're a believer, your slate is wiped clean daily. Each day I confess my sins (the things I did wrong) and start fresh. Then, my responsibility is to draw closer to God and work on not making those mistakes again, out of love for him. Christ has already secured my place with God for eternity; my only tasks are to help others, love others as Christ commanded, and not do things that separate me from God. In short, my job is to be *real*—with myself and with Christ.

Today, even through my daily struggles, I have a baseline peace when things go right and also when things go wrong. Why? Because I now believe that there is a plan for my life and the lives of those I love, and I believe God opens and shuts doors all the time for my good. My life's worth is not in my earthly successes but in my relationship with Christ and God and their love for me. They instill me with worth without me doing a thing. And so it is with every person. You are loved and valued, without doing a thing. Quite a concept, right?

Takeaway for the Searcher
There is nothing you have done that disqualifies you from God's love—*nothing*. You are as deserving as any nun or minister when it comes to God's grace and every bit as important to our Lord.

Takeaway for the Christian
If you are a new believer, expect some bumps in the road. That's okay—just stay real! Bring it all to God: the good, the bad, and the ugly. If you are a more experienced Christian, help those newer to the faith navigate their new reality.

CHAPTER 14

Things I've Seen

God creates miracles all the time. I have seen some of these miracles and the unique way in which God works. Once I left the "land of pretend" and really met Christ, I could see these past miracles more clearly than ever and recognize new ones, too.

I have seen God enable people to do what they couldn't do alone. My sister, Carole, has had a chronic illness for almost thirty years, one that has never been properly diagnosed. She has seen dozens and dozens of doctors and therapists and has struggled through the depression, exhaustion, and unique type of anxiety that comes with chronic disease. But I have seen her grow in her faith, despite not having answers for her health issues. And she continuously expresses a deep thoughtfulness and compassion for others who struggle with physical ailments because she knows just how hard each day can be. Carole has a childhood friend who suffered a traumatic brain injury in her teens and is confined to a wheelchair and largely unable to speak. For years, until Carole's own health worsened, she visited this friend and encouraged her. While other friends fell away, busy with their own lives, my sister remained constant. I praise God for Carole's life and her ministry of care for others.

Furthermore, I have witnessed our family's ongoing spiritual development as a result of my sister's illness. In the past I tended to despair about my sister's condition and be angry at God for allowing her to suffer, but now I have reached a level of trust about it. My parents' faith has also grown as they have watched their daughter struggle. We have become better people because of my sister, and we know firsthand what a blessing good health is. We never take it for granted. For our whole family, my sister's illness has highlighted the importance of life's little blessings. Remember that idea about a life full of meaning? We continue our daily prayers for her complete and total recovery and still believe she will be healed, in God's time.

I have seen God inspire growth in my husband, too. Sadly, he lost his father when he was just eight years old. When we were first married, Fred was angry with God for taking his father—a completely normal reaction after having to grow up without a dad. Today, I see my husband more at peace with his father's passing, and I have been fortunate and blessed to watch him grow into a loving, watchful, and very involved father himself. God worked his father's passing for good in his life and turned his hurt into a promise to himself to be the best father he could be. We both look forward to being with his earthly father in heaven someday.

I myself have experienced God in several additional ways. First, there is my love for my children. I was the type that never wanted to get married and definitely didn't want to have kids. But through my husband, my three sons, and my new daughter-in-law, I have seen how rich family life can be. Did I want this, initially? No. Can I imagine life without any of them? No.

Also, I have experienced the lively and custom-tailored way God answers prayers. About ten years ago, even as a committed follower of the faith, I was in a rut. It happens. I was bored and unhappy and couldn't find my way out of it. My children were growing up, and it seemed like they no longer needed me.

I was also in a drought in my prayer life. Prayers that had begun earnestly eventually trailed off into my staring into space, and I couldn't feel God's presence anywhere near me. This also happens, and it is hard to go through. It is important to note that all really important relationships hit dry spells—our daily lives on earth are not static but are like the tides, sometimes receding, and always moving, always changing.

I was not being a mature believer during my "drought" but was instead looking around at my externals—my house, my marriage, and my daily life—and finding fault. "What should I do?" I mused as I flopped around in my sweatshirt or house robe. Go to marriage counseling, get a better part-time job than the one I had, beg the boys to spend more time with me, or take a trip alone, perhaps? God could have done anything he wanted with my angst, but he did something amazing. He sent a horse.

That's right; during an antiquing trip alone in New Hampshire, he made sure I stumbled on one particular antique, an actual, real, live, broken-down old carriage horse whose best galloping days, I was assured, were behind him. I purchased him for a few hundred dollars on a whim and spent the next five happy years caring for him, riding him, and meeting a whole new community of fellow horse lovers. God knew that what I had needed was to get outside myself and do some good old-fashioned hard work. I needed to stop looking to everyone else to make me happy and let God teach me to be more independent and more adventurous, instead of depending on everyone else for my own satisfaction. That horse, now deceased, was one of the great blessings of my life.

As God did with me through my horse purchase, he has encouraged soldiers, blessed newlyweds, given adventurers courage, and mended the broken-hearted. His ways are a mystery, and although it is very human to question him, you must remember that we see only half the picture. We don't have a God's-eye view of our lives. To illustrate this for yourself, imagine choosing your career at age five. You don't know enough of your future story to ever be able to make that decision at that age. In the same way, we don't know how God takes the billions of strands of our lives, full of happiness and pain, gain and loss, laughter and tears, and works them like an artist to create something beautiful in the final analysis.

So, now what? You may find yourself interested enough to begin your own journey and willing to give God a try. But how exactly do you do that?

The first step you can take is simple: pray. Believe that you are being heard and tell God you are beginning this journey. You don't have to promise him anything, but ask for a few different things: Ask him to point you in the right direction. Ask him to bring a real believer into your life, one who won't pressure you but will listen thoughtfully and speak wisely. Ask God to illuminate the Bible for you, so that when you read it you will be able to feel the message pertaining to you, in other words "speaking" to you.

The second step is to decide about faith for yourself. This is the most important decision you will ever make in life, and as I shared at the beginning of this book, Christianity is under attack. There are many in this world who scoff at those who believe. There are many who deem believers to be not as smart or sophisticated as those like themselves, who shun faith in favor of intellectualism and only that which is provable. But I encourage you to stay strong; you have every right to investigate what is right for you. Remember, someone who is genuinely secure in their beliefs will not be threatened by your delving into a searching relationship with Christ. Most importantly, if you are on this journey to find Christ, know that there are others out there, all over the world in fact, who love him with all their hearts. His love allows us to love you and continue praying for your best outcome, even if you decide against Christianity. But I sure hope you don't. Another life is just waiting for you, right around the corner. . . Come and grab it!

Bible Passages to Get You Started

1. Remember the Bible verse I didn't know all those years ago at the "Bible Trivia" get-together? It is one of the most well-known verses, John chapter 3, verse 16: "For God so loved the world that he gave his one and only Son, that whoever believes in him shall not perish but have eternal life." This is what became very clear to me, during my moment of revelation. I now saw this as fact, not fantasy. God gave his son for us, so that we can one day be with him in heaven.

2. "'For I know the plans I have for you,' declares the LORD, 'plans to prosper you and not to harm you, plans to give you hope and a future'" (Jer. 29:11). This verse speaks to God's intimate interest in and knowledge of your life—the whole arc of your life, from conception through death, and into eternity. He wants to provide only good things for you and give you a future beyond your own imagining.

3. "For I am convinced that neither death nor life, neither angels nor demons, neither the present nor the future, nor any powers, neither height nor depth, nor anything else in all creation, will be able to separate us from the love of God that is in Christ Jesus our Lord" (Rom. 8:38-39). This verse speaks to God's absolute strength and power when it comes to his love for us. Neither the natural *nor* the supernatural can separate us from the love of God, expressed through his son Jesus. How comforting this passage is!

4. "Jesus answered, 'I am the way and the truth and the life. No one comes to the Father except through me'" (John 14:6). Jesus was answering his disciple Thomas in this passage, after he had asked Jesus how they (the disciples)

were to know their way forward without him. Jesus is also speaking to each one of us, today. This is also a very specific passage about the crucial nature of Christ; you cannot reach God without Christ.

5. "God is our refuge and strength, an ever-present help in trouble" (Pss. 46:1).This verse promises that you never, ever walk alone. God will be with you and help you through any situation, heartache, or loss.

6. "For the Spirit God gave us does not make us timid, but gives us power, love, and self-discipline" (2 Tim. 1:7). Christians are not shrinking violets! We conduct our lives with confidence, focus, and purpose, knowing God is watching us and will continually help us.

7. "The second is this: Love your neighbor as yourself. There is no commandment greater than these" (Mark 12:31). This passage tells us how important it is to love other human beings. The first commandment referenced in this passage is to love God with all our heart, all our soul, and all our might. This second directive is crystal clear; we are here to love each other.

8. "Do not be anxious about anything, but in every situation, by prayer and petition, with thanksgiving, present your requests to God" (Phil. 4:6).

Anxiety and stress are ever-present in modern life. We can give our cares to God, freeing our own hearts and minds. We can ask God for help and for all the things that we need, for our bodies and for our spirits, and know he is listening. He wants us to be grateful to him, to lean on him, and to be in closest communication with him always.

Remember, life is all about love, in the end.

"Amazing Grace"
by John Newton

- 1 -

Amazing grace! How sweet the sound,
That saved a wretch like me!
I once was lost, but now am found;
Was blind, but now I see.

- 2 -

'Twas grace that taught my heart to fear,
And grace my fears relieved;
How precious did that grace appear
The hour I first believed!

- 3 -

Through many dangers, toils, and snares,
I have already come;
'Tis grace that brought me safe thus far,
And grace will lead me home.

- 4 -

The Lord hath promised good to me,
His Word my hope secures;
He will my Shield and Portion be
As long as life endures.

- 5 -

Yea, when this flesh and heart shall fail,
And mortal life shall cease,
I shall possess, within the veil,
A life of joy and peace.

- 6 -

The earth shall soon dissolve like snow,
The sun forbear to shine;
But God, who called me here below,
Will be forever mine.

- 7 -

When we've been there ten thousand years,
Bright shining as the sun,
We've no less days to sing God's praise
Than when we'd first begun.

About the Author

D eirdre Reilly is a writer and journalist whose work on family, faith, politics, and parenting has been carried by national publications including *Fox News*, *Dallas Morning News*, *Hartford Courant*, *Boston Herald*, and others.

She has authored a long-running, nationally syndicated family humor column, co-hosted the *Family Talk* radio show on WBIX in Boston, and wrote the 2001 title *Exhausted Rapunzel: Tales of Modern Castle Life*. She has also been both a radio and television guest for her commentary on modern-day parenting, faith, and politics.

Deirdre lives outside Boston, Massachusetts, with her husband, Fred, and their youngest son, James, as well as three dogs, one cat, and their tortoise, Gary.

Endnotes

1.   Bill Flavell, "Eight Reasons Christianity Is False," Atheist Alliance International, July 23, 2018, https://www.atheistalliance.org/thinking-out-loud/eight-reasons-christianity-is-false/.

2.   C. S. Lewis, Mere Christianity (New York: Collier, 1952), 56.

3.   Whitney Hopler, "5 Lessons on Wonder From St. Patrick," Thrive Global, Thrive Global.com, March 14, 2017, https://thriveglobal.com/stories/5-lessons-on-wonder-from-st-patrick/.

Printed in the United States
By Bookmasters